PHOTOGRAPHY

Preserving the Past

These and other books are included in the
Encyclopedia of Discovery and Invention series:

PHOTOGRAPHY
Preserving the Past

by BRADLEY STEFFENS

The ENCYCLOPEDIA of
D·I·S·C·O·V·E·R·Y
and **INVENTION**

P.O. Box 289011 SAN DIEGO, CA 92198-0011

Library of Congress Cataloging-in-Publication Data

Steffens, Bradley, 1956–
  Photography : preserving the past / by Bradley Steffens.
    p. cm.— (The Encyclopedia of discovery and invention)
  Includes bibliographical references and index.
  Summary: Examines the history and development of photography and its technology and the role of photography in documenting current history.
  ISBN 1-56006-212-6
  1. Photography—History—Juvenile literature. [1. Photography—History.]
I. Title. II. Series.
TR149.S688   1991
770'.9—dc20   91-15570

Contents

■■■

Foreword

The belief in progress has been one of the dominant forces in Western Civilization from the Scientific Revolution of the seventeenth century to the present. Embodied in the idea of progress is the conviction that each generation will be better off than the one that preceded it. Eventually, all peoples will benefit from and share in this better world. R.R. Palmer, in his *History of the Modern World,* calls this belief in progress "a kind of nonreligious faith that the conditions of human life" will continually improve as time goes on.

For over a thousand years prior to the seventeenth century, science had progressed little. Inquiry was largely discouraged, and experimentation, almost nonexistent. As a result, science became regressive and discovery was ignored. Benjamin Farrington, a historian of science, characterized it this way: "Science had failed to become a real force in the life of society. Instead there had arisen a conception of science as a cycle of liberal studies for a privileged minority. Science ceased to be a means of transforming the conditions of life." In short, had this intellectual climate continued, humanity's future would have been little more than a clone of its past.

Fortunately, these circumstances were not destined to last. By the seventeenth and eighteenth centuries, Western society was undergoing radical and favorable changes. And the changes that occurred gave rise to the notion that progress was a real force urging civilization forward. Surpluses of consumer goods were replacing substandard living conditions in most of Western Europe. Rigid class systems were giving way to social mobility. In nations like France and the United States, the lofty principles of democracy and popular sovereignty were being painted in broad, gilded strokes over the fading canvasses of monarchy and despotism.

But more significant than these social, economic, and political changes, the new age witnessed a rebirth of science. Centuries of scientific stagnation began crumbling before a spirit of scientific inquiry that spawned undreamed of technological advances. And it was the discoveries and inventions of scores of men and women that fueled these new technologies, dramatically increasing the ability of humankind to control nature—and, many believed, eventually to guide it.

It is a truism of science and technology that the results derived from observation and experimentation are not finalities. They are part of a process. Each discovery is but one piece in a continuum bridging past and present and heralding an extraordinary future. The heroic age of the Scientific Revolution was simply a start. It laid a foundation upon which succeeding generations of imaginative thinkers could build.

It kindled the belief that progress is possible as long as there were gifted men and women who would respond to society's needs. When Antonie van Leeuwenhoek observed *Animalcules* (little animals) through his high-powered microscope in 1683, the discovery did not end there. Others followed who would call these "little animals" bacteria and, in time, recognize their role in the process of health and disease. Robert Koch, a German bacteriologist and winner of the Nobel Prize in Physiology and Medicine, was one of these men. Koch firmly established that bacteria are responsible for causing infectious diseases. He identified, among others, the causative organisms of anthrax and tuberculosis. Alexander Fleming, another Nobel Laureate, progressed still further in the quest to understand and control bacteria. In 1928, Fleming discovered penicillin, the antibiotic wonder drug. Penicillin, and the generations of antibi-

otics that succeeded it, have done more to prevent premature death than any other discovery in the history of humankind. And as civilization hastens toward the twenty-first century, most agree that the conquest of van Leeuwenhoek's "little animals" will continue.

The Encyclopedia of Discovery and Invention examines those discoveries and inventions that have had a sweeping impact on life and thought in the modern world. Each book explores the ideas that led to the invention or discovery, and, more importantly, how the world changed and continues to change because of it. The series also highlights the people behind the achievements—the unique men and women whose singular genius and rich imagination have altered the lives of everyone. Enhanced by photographs and clearly explained technical drawings, these books are comprehensive examinations of the building blocks of human progress.

PHOTOGRAPHY

Preserving the Past

PHOTOGRAPHY

Introduction

Tunneling through a crumbling burial mound in the ancient Mayan city of Dos Pilas in April 1991, an American archeologist named Arthur M. Demarest suddenly came upon a stone wall. Demarest was excited. For months, he had been searching for the tomb of an important Mayan leader known as Leader 2. At last, Demarest felt near his goal. Carefully, he removed a single stone from the wall. "It was scary because of the danger of collapse," the scientist later said. Using shaving mirrors, Demarest rigged up a simple periscope, fitted it into the hole, and peered inside. It appeared to be the tomb. Immediately, Demarest took out his camera, aimed it into the periscope, and began taking pictures.

Demarest wanted to preserve exactly how the burial chamber appeared when he found it, before it was disturbed or damaged. Like millions before him, he trusted photography to do the job. Since its invention nearly 170 years ago, photography has become the main way in which people record the present to preserve the past.

Thanks to photography, people today can look upon the faces of prominent leaders, great artists, exciting athletes, and other important people who lived years before. Likewise, people in the future will be able to look at photographs

TIMELINE: PHOTOGRAPHY

1 ▸ 2 ▸ 3 ▸ 4 ▸ 5 ▸ 6 ▸ 7 ▸ 8 ▸ 9 ▸ 10 ▸ 1

1 ■ 500 B.C.
Aristotle describes pinhole images.

2 ■ A.D. 1035
Ibn al-Haitham experiments with pinhole images.

3 ■ 1558
Giovanni Battista della Porta popularizes the camera obscura in *Magiae Naturalis*.

4 ■ 1614
Angelo Sala notes blackening of silver nitrate.

5 ■ 1727
Johann Heinrich Schulze stencils images into silver nitrate.

6 ■ 1777
Carl Wilhelm Scheele discovers why silver nitrate turns dark when exposed to light.

7 ■ 1802
Thomas Wedgwood makes images on paper with light.

8 ■ 1822
Joseph Nicéphore Niépce makes first photoengravings.

9 ■ 1824
Niépce takes first photograph from nature.

10 ■ 1834
William Henry Fox Talbot makes first photogenic drawings.

11 ■ 1837
Jacques Mandé Daguerre makes first photograph using silver iodide.

12 ■ 1839
Alphonse Giroux produces daguerreotype cameras.

13 ■ 1840
Josef Max Petzval computes design of new lens that permits sixteen times more light to enter camera.

taken today to learn more about our time. Photography is a window on the past.

Photography is also a telescope, bringing distant objects near. Pictures in books, magazines, and newspapers portray faraway people, animals, buildings, and landscapes. Much of what we know about the world we learn through photography.

Photography also reveals things that are too small, too distant, or moving too quickly to see with the naked eye. Using photography, scientists have been able to record the existence of particles that are smaller than atoms. They have also located stars, galaxies, and other objects that are millions of light-years away.

They have stopped hummingbirds in midflight. Photography enlarges our visual world.

At one time, the still camera was the only machine people had for recording visual images. Today, many different technologies are used for this purpose—motion pictures, videotape, and holograms among them. Even so, photography retains its importance. More people own cameras than ever before, taking more than fifty billion photographs a year worldwide. Each image is unique, preserving a single moment in time—a moment that has passed and can never be again. The photograph holds that moment near, granting the imaginative viewer entrance to a vanished world.

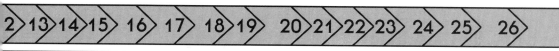

14 ■ 1847
Claude Félix Abel Niepce de St. Victor invents glass-plate photography.

15 ■ 1851
Frederick Scott Archer invents wet-plate process.

16 ■ 1861
Abraham Lincoln permits photographer Mathew B. Brady to visit battlefields of Civil War.

17 ■ 1873
The Daily Graphic publishes first newspaper photograph.

18 ■ 1884
Eastman introduces first roll film.

19 ■ 1888
Eastman begins to sell Kodak camera.

20 ■ 1925
Ernst Leitz company introduces the compact Leica camera.

21 ■ 1930
Clyde Tombaugh uses camera to discover Pluto.

22 ■ 1936
First issue of *Life* magazine published by Henry Luce.

23 ■ 1938
The Eastman Kodak Company begins to sell the first low-cost color film.

24 ■ 1948
Edwin H. Land introduces first instant picture camera.

25 ■ 1959
Soviet space probe *Luna 1* takes first close-up pictures of the moon.

26 ■ 1988
Canon Corporation introduces Xapshot, first digital imaging still camera for home use.

Darkened Rooms

Working alone in a darkened room of the Azhar mosque in Egypt around A.D. 1035, a scientist named Ibn al-Haitham carefully set up an experiment using several candles and an opaque screen. The experiment was designed to help answer a question al-Haitham had struggled with for several years, namely, "What is light?"

Unanswered Questions

Born in Basra, Iraq, and educated in the great libraries of Baghdad, the seventy-year-old scientist had studied everything the ancient Greek scholars—including

The Greek philosopher Aristotle noted that when sunlight passes through a pinhole, it forms an image of the sun on the ground.

Ptolemy, a second-century Greek astronomer and mathematician, was one of the scholars whose writings perplexed Ibn al-Haitham, an eleventh-century Iraqi scientist.

Aristotle, Euclid, and Ptolemy—had written about light. Experience had shown him, however, that the Greeks had left many questions unanswered.

For example, Aristotle had noted that when sunlight passes through a small hole, a pinhole, it forms an image of the sun on the ground. By using a pinhole, Aristotle had reported, a person could view an eclipse without looking at the sun. Aristotle had pointed out that the image that appears on the ground is the reverse of the image in the sky. A crescent that appears on the left side of the sun during an eclipse will appear on the right side of the pinhole image on the ground. But Aristotle had not explained why.

To answer this and other questions, al-Haitham decided to review everything that was known about light, then investigate and experiment, "exercising caution in the drawing of conclusions." The scientist planned to support each of his findings with an experiment, a mathematical proof, or both. "We should take care in all that we judge and criticize that we seek the truth and not be swayed by opinions," he wrote.

Al-Haitham started out by defining light as a substance created by luminous objects and reflected by all others. He called the light given off by luminous objects primary light and the light reflected by objects secondary light. Both primary and secondary light, he wrote, travel in straight lines, known as rays, from every point of an illuminated surface.

Experimenting with Light

The experiment al-Haitham set up in the darkened room of the Azhar mosque was designed to prove his theory that light rays travel in straight lines. The scientist arranged the candles in a particular order on a table, then lit them one by one. At one end of the table, he hung the screen. He then stood behind the screen, away from the burning candles.

Al-Haitham knew that if he made a small hole, or aperture, in the screen, light from the candles would pass through the hole and form an image on the wall beyond, just as sunlight that passes through a pinhole creates an image on the ground.

He reasoned that if light travels in straight lines, then the rays from a candle placed on the left side of the pinhole would pass through the opening at an angle and strike the wall to the right of the hole. Rays from a candle on the right side of the pinhole would strike the wall to the left of the hole. As a result, the candles in the pinhole image would be in the reverse order of the candles on the table. In addition, the image would be upside down. Rays from the top of the candle flame would pass downward through the pinhole and strike the wall below the hole, while rays from the bottom of the flame would pass upward through the pinhole and strike the wall above the hole.

Al-Haitham made a pinhole in the screen, then studied the image that appeared on the wall. As expected, the image of the candles was reversed and upside down. The scientist had proven that light moves in straight lines. The great Arab scientist carefully recorded his findings in the book he was writing about light and optics entitled *Kitab al-Manazir.*

About two hundred years after al-Haitham's death in 1039, *Kitab al-Manazir* was translated into Latin, the language of learning in medieval Europe. Slowly, handwritten copies of *Kitab al-Manazir,* known in Latin as *Perspectiva,* began to circulate among the scholars of Europe.

The Camera Obscura Comes to Europe

One of the first Europeans to try the experiments described in *Perspectiva* was Leonardo da Vinci. The famous Italian scientist and artist was amazed to find that by using mirrors, lenses, and pinholes, he could make light play all kinds

AL-HAITHAM'S EXPERIMENT WITH LIGHT

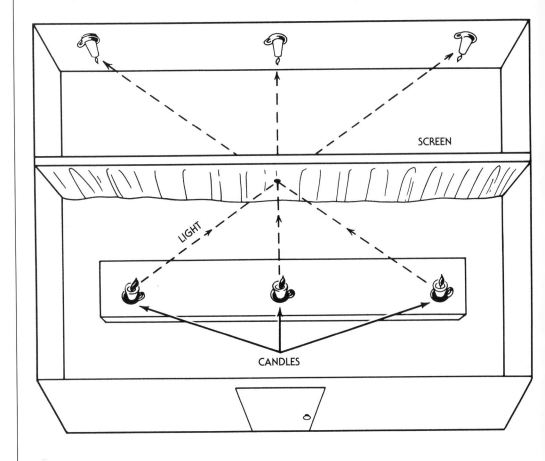

Iraqi Ibn al-Haitham's experiment with light in A.D. 1035 proved that light travels in a straight line. This creates some interesting illusions, as al-Haitham showed. He stretched a screen across the middle of a room, so that no light could pass through it except by way of one small hole in the middle of the screen. On one side of the screen, al-Haitham placed three lighted candles. Then he observed the images on the dark side of the room created by the candlelight that passed through the hole in the screen.

Al-Haitham reasoned that if light travels in a straight line, then light from the right side of the room would have to pass through the tiny hole in the screen and strike the opposite wall on the left side of the room. By the same principle, light coming from above the level of the hole would have to travel downward to pass through the hole, while light from below the hole must travel in an upward line to pass through it. As a result, an image of the half of the room lit by the candles would appear reversed and upside down on the wall on the other side of the screen.

of tricks. Around 1510, da Vinci made the following entry in his notebooks:

> When the images of illuminated objects pass through a small round hole into a very dark room...you will see on the paper all those objects in their natural shapes and colors. They will be reduced in size, and upside down, owing to the intersection of the rays at the aperture.

Because the Italian words for "darkened room" are *camera obscura,* these words began to be used as the name for any device used to create pinhole images.

In 1521, one of da Vinci's students, Cesare Cesariano, published the first European account of the camera obscura, but the most widely read description of the device appeared in 1558. This ac-

Leonardo da Vinci was one of the first Europeans to perform the experiments described in al-Haitham's Perspectiva. *Like al-Haitham, da Vinci was amazed and intrigued by the tiny pinhole images.*

count was written by an Italian nobleman name Giovanni Battista della Porta.

Born in Naples around 1535, della Porta belonged to a family that traced its noble blood back more than a thousand years to ancient Rome. Like most boys of his class, della Porta was raised to become an *otioso,* or "man of leisure." He was taught the arts, science, and religion by the finest private tutors in Naples.

Natural Magic

At the age of fifteen, della Porta began to collect unusual facts and stories about nature. The young scholar believed everything in nature is part of a perfectly ordered design. He reasoned that by exploring nature's secrets, he might glimpse the inner workings of this order, gaining a pure form of wisdom. He called such learning natural magic:

> There are two sorts of Magic: the one is infamous, and unhappy, because it hath to do with foul spirits, and consists of Inchantments and wicked Curiosity; and this is called Sorcery; an art which all learned men detest....The other Magic is natural; which all excellent men do admit and embrace, and worship with great applause....This Art, I say, is full of much virtue, of many secret mysteries; it openeth unto us the properties and qualities of hidden things, and the knowledge of the whole course of Nature.

Della Porta organized his findings into a book entitled *Magiae Naturalis,* or *Natural Magic.* In a section of the book entitled "Of Strange Glasses," della Porta described the camera obscura in detail:

> You must shut all the Chamber [room] windows, and it will do well to shut up all holes besides, lest any light

CAMERA OBSCURA

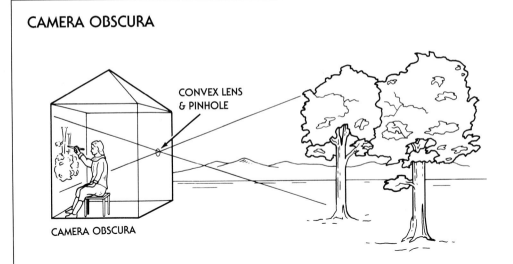

CONVEX LENS & PINHOLE

CAMERA OBSCURA

In the sixteenth century, men like Leonardo da Vinci and Giovanni Battista della Porta employed al-Haitham's principles of light to create the camera obscura, which means "darkened room" in Italian. They made specially designed dark rooms so that light from a brightly lit scene would pass through a pinhole in one wall of the room and create an upside down, reversed image of the scene on the opposite wall of the darkened room.

In 1558 della Porta showed that a convex lens placed over the pinhole can reduce a large scene to fit on the camera obscura wall and intensify the light so that the image appears brighter and clearer. From that time on, artists began using portable camera obscuras to produce realistic landscapes and other scenes. The first of these were tents, but by 1600 portable camera obscuras were being made from boxes with a focusing lens, so that the user could see the image in the camera obscura without actually having to be inside it.

breaking in should spoil all. Only make one hole...as great as your little finger: across from this, let there be white walls of paper, or white clothes, so shall you see all that is done [outside] in the Sun, and those that walk in the streets...and what is right will be the left, and all things changed.

An expert in the uses of mirrors and lenses, della Porta described how to magnify the image using a convex lens, a clear glass disk that is thick in the middle and thin at the edges. He also explained how to brighten the image and turn it right side up. The results, he wrote, were breathtaking:

> You shall presently see all things clearer, the countenances of men walking, the colors, Garments, and all things as if you stood [close] by; you shall see them with so much pleasure, that those that see it can never enough admire it.

Della Porta suggested that the camera obscura could be used to draw and paint scenes from nature with greater accuracy and realism. He described how an artist

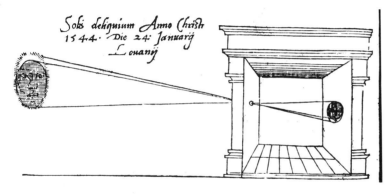

could use the camera obscura to project an image onto a sheet of paper. The artist could then draw around the patches of light with a pencil to outline the image, then fill in the picture with paint.

An Exciting Demonstration

When della Porta learned about the camera obscura, he was thrilled. This was natural magic of the highest order, and he could not wait to share it with others. He invited his friends and a few important citizens of Naples to his home for a private demonstration of his latest findings. Many of these people were members of the Accademia Secretorum Naturae, a scientific group della Porta had founded years before.

The wealthy nobleman decided to show off the device as dramatically as possible. He made a small hole in a wooden window shutter, then covered the opening. Next, he hired a troupe of actors to perform a pantomime outside the room, in line with the aperture.

On the day of the demonstration, della Porta's friends and acquaintances arrived at the scientist's home. When all were present, della Porta led his guests to the specially prepared room. The curtains were drawn, and the shutters were closed tight. All the chairs faced one wall—the wall opposite the hidden aperture. When his guests were seated, della Porta signaled the actors to begin the play, then closed the door. After a few words of introduction, he uncovered the aperture.

An early illustration of the camera obscura shows the image of a church reversed and inverted as light rays from its surface converge through an aperture.

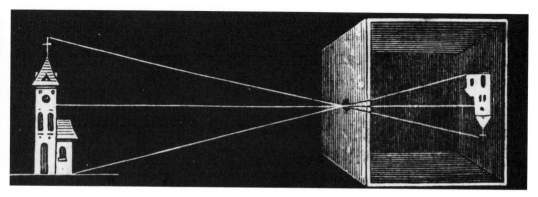

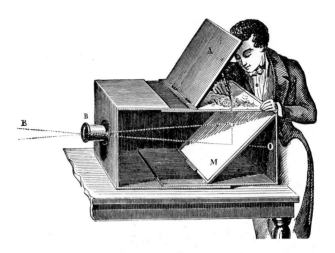

This eighteenth-century illustration shows an artist using a portable camera obscura as an aid in drawing.

Della Porta's guests were stunned by what they saw. Tiny human figures crawled across the wall in full color. Some in the group were fascinated, but others were frightened. They could think of only one explanation for what they saw: witchcraft. Some began to pray aloud. Others rushed from the room, cursing their host.

Della Porta was crushed. His moment of glory was ruined. But that was only the beginning. The scientist's activities were reported to the leaders of the Catholic Church. Soon afterward, della Porta was summoned to appear before a religious court. The charge was sorcery, a crime punishable by death. Della Porta was able to convince the court of the difference between sorcery and natural magic, but the church still banned the publication of his work for six years.

Although della Porta's work was suppressed in Italy, *Magiae Naturalis* was translated and published throughout Europe. Soon, scientists were showing the camera obscura to important people in every country. Delighted by what they saw, many leaders ordered that camera obscuras be added to buildings in their cities as a kind of novelty. Camera obscuras in Bristol, England; Edinburgh, Scotland; and elsewhere are still in use today.

Improvements in the Camera Obscura

A few scientists suggested further improvements in the device. A German mathematics professor named Daniel Schwenter placed a lens at either end of a hole drilled through a wooden ball. He fitted it into a socket within a window shutter that had been closed to darken the room. Schwenter's ball, known as an ox-eye, admitted a small amount of light into the room. The ball could be turned to focus images from any direction onto the opposite wall. The German artist Hans Hauer used this device as an aid when drawing a panoramic view of the city of Nuremberg around 1635.

Although the ox-eye widened the view of the camera obscura, the device was still limited to what could be seen from a single room. But scientists had already provided the means to overcome this limitation. As early as 1580, a scientist named Friedrich Risner suggested how to build a portable camera obscura. When his idea was published in 1606, it inspired artists and scientists to design all kinds of camera obscuras that could be packed up and moved around.

The most popular portable camera obscuras were collapsible tents. These were large enough to contain a folding chair and small drawing table for the artist. The aperture of the device was at the end of a tube that projected from the top of the tent like a periscope. A mirror reflected the image down the tube, through the focusing lenses, and onto the drawing table below.

The next step was to build a camera obscura that could be used without climbing inside. A German monk named Johann Zahn designed a camera obscura that was just nine inches high and twenty-four inches long. It had an adjustable focus, an adjustable aperture, and a small mirror inside that reflected the image up to a ground-glass viewing screen. Zahn's design for a portable camera obscura would not change for nearly two hundred years.

Chemistry Points the Way to Photography

About the time the portable camera obscura was being developed, an Italian doctor named Angelo Sala made a discovery destined to change the use of the device forever.

Around 1610, Sala began to make and prescribe medicines, believing "that they have a force...that resists the disease." Like della Porta, da Vinci, al-Haitham, and others before him, Sala valued direct experience more than ancient traditions. He attacked the typical doctor of his day for not being willing to "deviate a hair's breadth from his opinions, no matter whether he was right or wrong."

Sala's work with medicine led him to a general interest in chemistry. He was the first known chemist to confirm the makeup of a substance by breaking it into its basic parts. He distilled vitriol, a sulfuric acid, into three substances: "copper ore, sulfur fumes, and water."

In 1614, Sala turned his attention to chemicals known as silver salts. As he worked with one of these chemicals, silver nitrate, he noticed something unusual. "When you expose silver nitrate to the sun, it turns black as ink," he noted in his papers.

Sala's discovery meant that light could be used like a paintbrush to darken a canvas of silver salts. But the idea of creating an image with light and silver salts never occurred to Sala. He had discovered the chemical basis of photography, but his finding went unused for over one hundred years.

Images Made by Light

Finally, in 1727, a professor of medicine at the University of Altdorf in Germany observed the same phenomenon Sala had written about in 1614. Johann Heinrich Schulze noticed that a bottle containing a mixture of silver, nitric acid, and chalk, which normally appeared white, had turned dark purple after sitting a long time in the window of his laboratory.

When Schulze lifted the bottle to examine it, he noticed a swirl of white within the dark liquid. The swirl appeared near the label of the bottle. Carefully, Schulze peeled the label off the glass. The fluid behind the label was white.

Schulze was not sure what had turned the fluid dark or why it had remained white behind the label. He assumed that either heat or light from the sun had affected the chemical makeup of the fluid. To find out if heat had caused the change, Schulze placed a bottle of the fluid in an oven. When he removed it, the fluid was hot, but still white. He then placed a bottle near the window. This fluid turned dark. Schulze had proven that light, not heat, changed the color of the silver nitrate fluid.

Schulze was fascinated by the darkening of his silver nitrate solution. He made little paper cutouts of letters and shapes and pasted them to bottles containing the light-sensitive fluid. After the solution darkened in the sunlight, he peeled away the cutouts. Ghostly white silhouettes of the shapes floated in the fluid. Once exposed to the light, however, the white areas slowly turned black. Schulze was the first person in history to form images with light, but he was not able to prevent them from fading away.

Discovering Why Silver Images Turn Black

Like Sala, Schulze published the results of his silver nitrate experiments. Other scientists began to wonder why the sunlight turned the fluid black. The man who answered this question was a Swedish chemist and pharmacist named Carl Wilhelm Scheele.

Born in 1742, Scheele learned how to write chemical symbols and prescriptions at a very early age. As a teenager, Scheele disagreed with his teachers about the nature of fire, which was then considered an element, a pure substance. His experiments with fire led him to the most important discovery of his career: the existence of oxygen.

In 1770, Scheele began to experiment with silver salts. He found that different parts of the light spectrum affect silver salts differently. Blue light darkens silver nitrate greatly, while red light affects it less. In 1777, Scheele found out what happens when silver nitrate turns dark.

Silver nitrate is a compound, meaning that it is made up of more than one element. The elements in silver nitrate are silver, nitrogen, and oxygen. Scheele's experiments showed that light breaks these elements apart, separating the pure metallic silver from the nitrogen and oxygen. This chemical change caused the fluid to change color.

Experimenting with Silver and Light

Scheele's findings interested a young English potter who was looking for an easy way to copy pottery designs. The young man was Thomas Wedgwood, the son of the great English potter Josiah Wedgwood. Like many artists of his time, the younger Wedgwood owned a camera obscura, which he used to copy pottery designs onto paper.

What had not occurred to Sala, Schulze, or Scheele did occur to Wedgwood. He realized that the light from a camera obscura could be used to darken silver salts in a way that would record a visual image. Wedgwood coated a piece of paper with silver nitrate, placed it on the glass viewing surface of his camera obscura, and opened the aperture. The silver salts on the paper turned dark, but they did not record the image.

Thinking that the light reflected through the camera obscura might be too weak to leave a clear impression, Wedgwood decided to use direct sunlight. He placed a sheet of paper treated with silver nitrate under a piece of glass that had been painted with a design. He then laid the glass and paper in the sun. Later, he described what happened:

> When a white surface, covered with a solution of nitrate of silver, is placed behind a painting on glass exposed to the solar light, the rays transmitted through the differently painted surfaces produce distinct tints of brown or black, sensibly differing in intensity according to the shades of the picture, and where the light is unaltered, the colour of the nitrate becomes deepest.... After the colour has been once fixed upon the leather or paper, it cannot be removed by the application of water, or by water and soap, and it is in a high degree permanent.

The kind of image Wedgwood had produced would one day be known as a contact image, or contact print, because the object being recorded was placed in contact with the light-sensitive material that recorded its presence.

When Wedgwood wrote that the image was permanent, he meant that the image he created on paper could not easily be erased or washed away. When it came to fading, however, Wedgwood's process was no more permanent than Schulze's:

> The copy of a painting, or the profile, immediately after being taken, must be kept in an obscure place. It may indeed be examined in the shade, but in this case, the exposure should be only for a few minutes; by the light of candles or lamps, as commonly employed, it is not sensibly affected.

Thomas Wedgwood was able to form images with light using a method known as contact printing. These images faded when exposed to light, however.

The first person in history to create an image on paper using nothing but light and chemicals, Wedgwood knew he was on the verge of giving humanity a great new tool. Only one obstacle remained, he wrote in 1802: "Nothing but a method of preventing the unshaded parts of the image from being colored by exposure to the day is wanting to render the process as useful as it is elegant."

Wedgwood, who died just three years later, would not be the first person to find that method. The person who would lived a few hundred miles away, across the English Channel in a small village in France. That man's name was Joseph Nicéphore Niépce.

Permanent Images

Like Thomas Wedgwood, Joseph Nicé-phore Niépce wanted to find a way to copy pictures without drawing them by hand. A printer, Niépce knew a great deal about a new printing process known as lithography. He believed this process could be refined to record images directly from drawings. He was right.

Developed in 1796 by Alois Sene-felder of Germany, lithography used chemicals to control the placement of ink on the printing surface. Knowing that water and oil do not mix, Sene-felder had drawn images on a printing plate with a waxy material similar to a crayon, then dampened the surface with water. He then coated the plate with oily ink. The ink stuck to the waxy areas but was repelled by the wet areas. When the paper was pressed against the plate, it absorbed the ink from the waxy areas, duplicating the drawing.

Looking for a Way to Copy with Light

Niépce was convinced that a lithographic surface could be prepared for printing by exposing it to light. He reasoned that if a surface were coated with light-sensitive materials, light could arrange these chemicals into the desired image.

Around 1816, Niépce began to test this theory. He started coating printing plates of zinc, copper, glass, and pewter with different substances. He then focused light on the plates, using a camera

obscura. The light caused a noticeable change in some chemicals, but the effects were faint and fleeting.

Joseph Nicéphore Niépce is recognized as the first person to create permanent images with light.

In 1820, Niépce's search for a method of drawing with light became more urgent. In his printing shop, Niépce employed his son, Isidore, to copy drawings onto the printing plates. When the young man was called upon to serve in the French army, Joseph Niépce began to worry. He knew he did not have the talent to copy the drawings himself. Without his son, his business was in trouble. Niépce began to work even harder on his new method of duplicating images.

For two years, Niépce searched for a mixture of chemicals that would respond quickly and strongly to the action of light. Around 1822, he began to succeed. He found that if he dissolved bitumen of Judea, a kind of asphalt, into certain solvents, he could create a varnish that turned hard when exposed to light. This suited his purpose exactly.

To try out his copying process, Niépce decided to make a kind of contact print. He soaked an engraving of the Virgin Mary in oil to make the paper translucent. Next he laid the engraving on a pewter plate coated with his special varnish. Then he placed the plate in direct sunlight. As he had hoped, the light portions of the engraving let through enough sunlight to harden the varnish on the plate below. The dark portions of the engraving, however, kept the light from reaching the varnish. As a result, the varnish in these areas remained soft.

Niépce removed the plate from the light and placed it into a bath of "one part lavender oil and six parts white mineral oil or petroleum." The softest portions of the varnish washed away, leaving small grooves in the surface of the plate exactly where the dark lines of the engraving had been. Niépce then placed the pewter plate into a bath of acids to etch the grooves deeply into the surface.

To print the image, Niépce coated the plate with ink, then wiped the surface clean with a soft cloth. As with a normal engraving surface, ink remained in the grooves of Niépce's specially prepared printing plate. When Niépce pressed the plate against a clean sheet of paper, the ink transferred to the paper, producing an exact copy of the original engraving.

Niépce called his new plate-making process heliogravure, combining the Greek word for "sun," *helios,* and the French word for "engraving," *gravure.* The heliographic plate Niépce produced in 1822 was the first permanent image created with light. For that reason, it is considered the world's first photograph.

The First Photo from Nature

When most people today think of a photograph, they picture a scene from everyday life, not a copy of a work of art. Although the image Niépce produced in 1822 was made with light, it does not match the popular notion of the photograph. An image he produced two years later, however, does.

In 1824, Niépce placed a pewter plate coated with his special varnish into a camera obscura. He set the camera in a window of his home at Saint-Loup-de-Varennes and opened the aperture. He left the box in place for a full eight hours. Slowly, the sun crossed the sky. Inch by inch, shadows crept across the courtyard outside. Inside Niépce's camera, the varnish on the pewter plate hardened.

HELIOGRAVURE

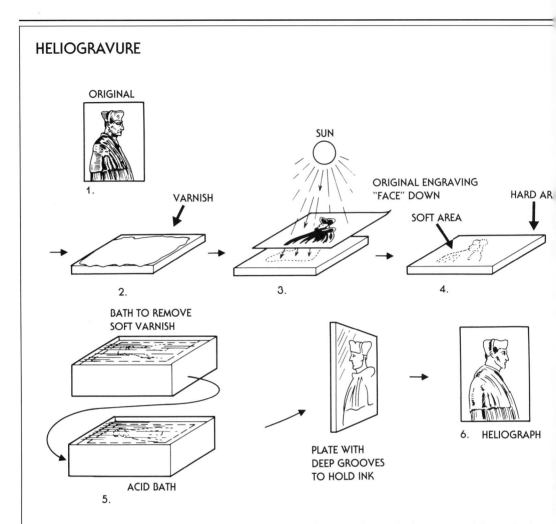

ORIGINAL

1.

VARNISH

2.

SUN

ORIGINAL ENGRAVING "FACE" DOWN

3.

HARD AR

SOFT AREA

4.

BATH TO REMOVE SOFT VARNISH

ACID BATH

5.

PLATE WITH DEEP GROOVES TO HOLD INK

6. HELIOGRAPH

Joseph Niépce produced the world's first permanent image created with light. Niépce called his image a heliogravure, literally a "sun engraving." The first step in his process was to select an ink engraving printed on paper and soak it in oil. This made the paper transparent, so that light passed through it wherever the paper was not covered by the inked lines of the engraving (1). Then he coated the surface of a pewter plate with a special varnish that hardened when exposed to light (2). Next, he covered the varnished plate with the oil-soaked engraving and set it in the sunlight (3). Since the sunlight could

only pass through the parts of the oiled paper that were not covered with ink, the varnish remained soft under the inked portions of the engraving but hardened everywhere else (4).

Niépce washed the soft varnish off the plate with a special oil bath, leaving shallow grooves wherever the ink had been on the original engraving. To make these grooves deeper, he placed the plate in an acid bath (5). The result was an engraved plate, which, when placed in a lithographic press, would print identical paper copies, or heliographs, of the original engraving (6).

Late in the afternoon, Niépce closed the aperture. He removed the pewter plate from the camera and dipped it into his chemical bath. The softest portions of the varnish melted away. The harder portions dissolved slightly, while the hardest portions remained unchanged. The result was a plate engraved to many different depths.

Niépce did not have to print from the plate to see the results of his experiment. As he turned the plate in his hand, light reflected from the different levels of the varnish, creating an image. When he tilted the plate at just the right angle, Niépce could see the outlines of buildings, roofs, and chimneys. Niépce held in his hand the world's first photograph from nature, and he had taken it.

Niépce sensed the importance of the moment, but he kept his discovery to himself. He wanted to improve his picture-taking method before he told anyone else about it.

Between 1824 and 1826, Niépce produced more images with light. Finally, he decided to travel to England to announce his breakthrough to the Royal Society, the scientific academy that met at the Royal Institution in London.

In 1827, Niépce appeared before the Royal Society bearing several sheets of paper and a pewter plate. He showed the scholars his heliographic prints and the plate that held what he called the "first successful effort at reproducing nature." The plate Niépce left with the Royal Society is the oldest surviving example of his work.

After making his announcement, Niépce returned to France to improve his picture-taking method. He worked in secret, mentioning his work only to the man who sold him optical equipment. As it turned out, this man, Charles Louis Chevalier, could not keep a secret.

The world's oldest photograph from nature: a view from the window of Niépce's home at Saint-Loup-de-Varennes, France.

Investigating Daguerre

The most famous maker of camera obscuras in France, Chevalier supplied optical equipment to a well-known stage designer in Paris named Louis Jacques Mandé Daguerre. Daguerre had become famous as one of the inventors of the diorama, a large-scale scenic view presented to an audience in a theater. Using translucent paintings and special lighting, Daguerre was able to produce spectacular, three-dimensional panoramas of the Swiss Alps and other famous scenes. Daguerre's dioramas were wildly popular among the people of Paris.

Chevalier knew that, like Niépce, Daguerre was working on a way to make lasting pictures with a camera obscura. On one of his visits to Paris, Chevalier told Daguerre of Niépce's breakthrough. Right away, Daguerre wrote a letter to Niépce. Daguerre described his own research and asked Niépce for help. Niépce wrote back, but he told Daguerre very little about his work. Meanwhile, Niépce wrote to a colleague in Paris to find out more about Daguerre:

> This gentleman, having been informed, I do not know to what extent, of the object of my researches, wrote to me last year…to let me know that for a long time he had occupied himself with the same object….I do not want to deceive you, Monsieur, that a seeming incoherence of his ideas has caused me not to tell him too much….Will you be good enough to send me your personal information on Daguerre and your opinion of him.

Niépce's colleague reported that Daguerre "has a rare intelligence for the things that deal with machines and

A well-known set designer, Louis Jacques Mandé Daguerre was fascinated by light and optics. His interest in making permanent pictures with light led him to write Joseph Niépce and propose partnership.

lighting effects." Reassured, Niépce continued to write Daguerre. In August of 1827, the two men met.

Although very different, the quiet scientist and the outgoing stage designer liked each other right away. They discussed their secret discoveries, trading ideas about how to make pictures with light. Eventually, Niépce and Daguerre formed a formal partnership to further develop the heliographic process.

The Struggles of Daguerre and Niépce

By the time he had met Niépce, Daguerre had already made progress in his efforts to produce lasting images with a camera obscura. Daguerre was interested in effects of iodine, a chemical that had been discovered in 1814. Although not sensitive to light, iodine bonds with silver to create a light-sensitive compound called silver iodide.

Daguerre and Niépce struggled for four years to find a way to make permanent images with silver iodide. They coated copper plates with pure silver, then exposed the plates to iodine vapors. The iodine bonded with the silver, creating an even coating of silver iodide. Daguerre and Niépce were surprised to find that this coating did not appear to change very much when exposed to the light of a camera obscura.

The two scientists had made very little progress when Niépce suddenly died of a stroke in 1833. Isidore Niépce took his father's place in the partnership, but it was left to Daguerre to find a way to finish the work he and the elder Niépce had begun.

New Success with Mercury

Daguerre guessed that the silver iodide on his plates was changing when exposed to light, but that these changes remained invisible, or latent. One day, Daguerre accidentally exposed one of his plates to the fumes of the chemical mercury. The mercury formed a shiny alloy with the silver in those places where light had struck the plate. As a result, the lightest portions of the image shone brightly. Where no light had reached the plate, no alloy formed. These areas remained dull. The result was a very clear image formed by reflections from the metal plate.

Daguerre realized that it did not take nearly as long to form a latent image as it did a visible one, so he began to test the effects of shorter exposure times. Using mercury to bring out the latent image, Daguerre found

he could produce a clear image with a twenty-minute exposure.

Daguerre was able to make pictures more quickly, but he could not make them last very long. Each time he viewed a plate, the light in the room caused more of the silver iodide to form an alloy with the mercury, clouding the original image. Daguerre needed to find something that would prevent the silver iodide from changing every time it was exposed to light.

After four years, Daguerre found a substance to "fix" silver iodide: sodium chloride, or common salt. The salt dissolved the silver iodide, leaving delicate shadings of the alloy on the bare silver plate. Viewed from the proper angle, the silver plate appeared black. On the dark background floated a brilliant image of whatever the camera had been focused on—flower, tree, or human being. In 1837, Daguerre made his first photograph using the new method, a view of his studio in Paris.

Announcing the Daguerreotype

Late in 1838, Daguerre approached the French scientist Francois Arago with a special request. He asked Arago to present samples of his work to the French Academy of Sciences. Daguerre wanted to announce his discovery to the world, but he was afraid that the scientists in the academy might ask questions that he could not answer. Arago agreed.

On January 7, 1839, Arago stood before a joint meeting of the Academy of Sciences and the Academy of Fine Arts. He held in his hands several small, mirrorlike objects. Each object had an image on one side. As Arago presented

(Left) One of Daguerre's early photographic images of a Paris street, taken in 1839. Because of Daguerre's pioneering work, the first photos were called "daguerreotypes." (Below) French scientist François Arago made the astounding new process of photography known to the world on January 7, 1839.

the objects, which he called daguerreotypes, to the members of the academy, murmurs of amazement filled the room.

A reporter for the *Journal of Franklin Institute* of Philadelphia wrote:

> [The members] were particularly struck with the marvelous minuteness of detail.... In one representing the Pont Marie, all the minutest indentations and divisions of the ground, of the buildings, the goods lying on the wharf, even the small stones under the water, were all shown with incredible accuracy. The use of a magnifying glass revealed an infinity of other details quite undistinguishable by the naked eye.

A reporter for a British publication, *The Penny Cyclopedia,* called the invention "little short of miraculous."

Millions of people around the world were stunned by the amazing news. For the first time in history, a machine could be used to produce an exact likeness of almost any object in nature. No one was more shocked by Daguerre's announcement than a little-known British scientist named William Henry Fox Talbot.

■ ■ ■ ■ ■ ■ ■ ■ ■ ■

CHAPTER 3

A New Art

William Henry Fox Talbot was at home in Wiltshire, England, when he heard about Daguerre's announcement. The news did more than surprise him, he later wrote. It "frustrated the hope" that had sustained him for "nearly five years" through "a long and complicated series of experiments—the hope, namely, of being the first to announce to the world the existence of a New Art"—photography.

At the time of Daguerre's announcement, Talbot had in his possession an unusual collection of small pictures on paper. The pictures portrayed objects Talbot had found around his home—a few feathers, a bit of lace, a wildflower. Each object was outlined in perfect detail. Talbot had made the pictures himself. He called them photogenic drawings, from the Greek words *photos*, meaning "light," and *genesis*, meaning "origin." As the name implied, the pictures had been made with light. They were photographs.

Talbot's Breakthrough

Talbot had made his first photogenic drawings in the spring of 1834, a full five years before Daguerre's announcement. Talbot told the story of his breakthrough this way:

> One of the first days of the month of October 1833, I was amusing myself on the lovely shores of the Lake of

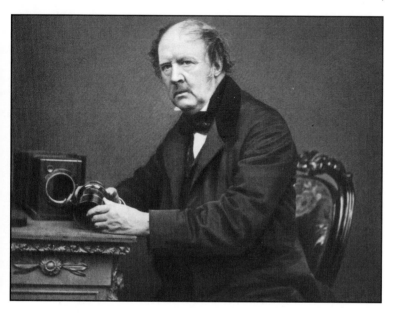

William Henry Fox Talbot was shocked to hear about the invention of the daguerreotype. He had been making photogenic drawings for nearly five years and had hoped to be "the first to announce to the world the existence of a New Art."

Como, in Italy, taking sketches.... I then thought of trying again a method which I had tried many years before ...to take a Camera Obscura, and throw the image of the objects on a piece of transparent tracing paper laid upon a pane of glass in the focus of the instrument.... It was during these thoughts that the idea occurred to me ...how charming it would be if it were possible to cause these natural images to imprint themselves durably, and remain fixed upon the paper! And since, according to chemical writers, the nitrate of silver is a substance peculiarly sensitive to the action of light, I resolved to make a trial of it.

More Experiments with Silver and Light

Talbot returned to England in January 1834 and at once began his experiments. He moistened a sheet of writing paper with a salt solution, then allowed it to dry. He then coated the paper with a so-lution of silver nitrate. When the paper had dried a second time, Talbot exposed it to sunlight. The paper turned dark as expected, but it did so very slowly. "I was disappointed to find," Talbot wrote, "that the effect was very slowly produced in comparison with what I had anticipated."

Talbot then tried coating a sheet with silver chloride. Again he was disappointed. "This was found no better than the other, turning slowly to a darkish violet colour when exposed to the sun," he wrote.

Although discouraged with his results, Talbot persisted. In one attempt, he mixed his moistening solution with less salt than usual. The results were dramatic. "This paper, when exposed to the sunshine, immediately manifested a far greater degree of sensitiveness than I had witnessed before," wrote Talbot, "the whole of the surface turning black uniformly and rapidly: establishing at once and beyond all question the important fact that a lesser quantity of salt produced a greater effect."

An early photogenic drawing by Talbot features a few feathers, leaves, and a bit of lace.

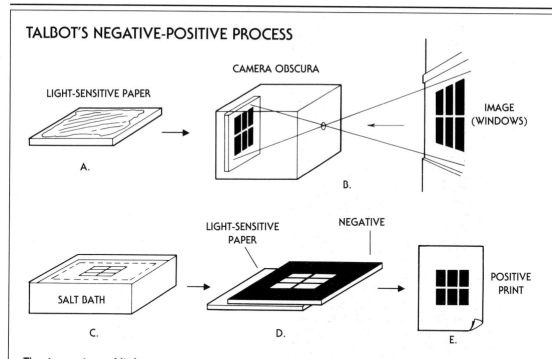

The invention of light-sensitive paper by William Henry Fox Talbot in 1834, along with his process of converting a negative image to a positive one, began the modern era of photography. Talbot produced the first light-sensitive paper by soaking a sheet of paper in a salt solution and then coating it with silver nitrate (A). After placing this paper inside a camera obscura and exposing it to a scene (B), he fixed the paper by bathing it in a strong salt solution. This washed away the unexposed silver nitrate (C).

The image that remained on the paper was darkest wherever the silver nitrate had been exposed to the most light, and lightest where it had been exposed to the least light. In other words, it was just the opposite of the original subject. Talbot called this a negative. By placing the negative over another sheet of light-sensitive paper and exposing it to light (D), he produced another image that looked exactly like the original subject. This he called a positive (E). The great advantage of Talbot's negative-positive process for developing photographs is that an unlimited number of positives can be made from a single negative.

Making Lasting Images on Paper

Once he had produced a light-sensitive paper, Talbot tried to form an image on it. Like Schulze, Wedgwood, and Niépce, Talbot began by making contact prints. "In the spring of 1834," he wrote, "no difficulty was found in obtaining distinct and very pleasing images of such things as leaves, lace, and other flat objects of complicated outlines, by exposing them to the light of the sun."

Talbot's experience with salt solutions led him to solve the one problem Wedgwood had not been able to overcome: how to stop the darkening of the

In 1835, Talbot was able to reduce the time needed to obtain an image in bright sunlight to ten minutes. A person who was the subject of such a picture, such as Talbot's gamekeeper, could not move while the picture was taken, or the image would be blurred.

Talbot's friend, Michael Faraday, the English chemist and physicist, presented Talbot's photogenic drawings to the Royal Society of Science just three weeks after Daguerre's announcement.

exposed image on paper. Talbot reasoned that if using less salt in his solution sped up the darkening process, then using more salt might slow or even halt it. To "fix" his images, Talbot bathed his photographs in a strong salt solution.

Once he could make lasting images, Talbot decided to try out the idea he had thought of on the shores of Lake Como.

He sensitized a piece of paper about one and a half inches square and placed it in a small camera obscura of his own design. Later, he described the result:

> During the brilliant summer of 1835 in England I made new attempts to obtain pictures of buildings with the Camera Obscura; and having devised a process which gave additional sensibility to the paper...by giving it alternate washes of salt and silver, and using it in a moist state, I succeeded in reducing the time necessary for obtaining an image with the Camera Obscura on a bright day to ten minutes.

Ten years before, Joseph Nicéphore Niépce had placed a camera obscura in a window of his home to take the first permanent photograph from nature. In August 1835, Talbot aimed his camera at a window of his castle, Lacock Abbey, and took the oldest surviving photograph on paper, *Latticed Window*.

Perfecting the New Art

Talbot continued making photogenic drawings for four years. He built more of his small cameras and placed them around his home to take more pictures.

Stumbling upon the small wooden boxes in all sorts of odd places, Talbot's wife began to jokingly refer to her husband's cameras as "mousetraps." The nickname was apt. Talbot's boxes were indeed little traps, not for mice, of course, but for light.

A member of the Royal Society of Science, Talbot could have presented his photographs to the world years before Daguerre did, but he had decided to wait until he had further perfected his process. When word of Daguerre's announcement reached him, Talbot instantly regretted his decision. Unaware that Niépce had taken the world's first photograph fifteen years earlier, Talbot believed he may have been the first to develop the new art. He knew, however, that since he had not announced his findings, he could not receive credit for the invention. Still, the gentleman scientist wanted the world to know that he had developed a method of making pictures with light that was quite different from Daguerre's.

Talbot contacted his friend Michael Faraday, the great English scientist. Faraday quickly arranged for a showing of Talbot's photogenic drawings at the Royal Institution in London. On January 25, 1839, less than three weeks after Daguerre's announcement, members of the Royal Society got their first look at Talbot's photogenic drawings. Among those present was the English chemist and astronomer Sir John Herschel. "It is a miracle," Herschel declared after seeing Talbot's images.

Herschel also proposed the name for the new art: photography. He derived the term from the Greek words *photos,* meaning "light," and *graphos,* meaning "to draw." Talbot and others agreed that "to draw with light" was an apt way to describe the new process. When Talbot published the world's first book of photographs in 1843, he called it *The Pencil of Nature.*

On January 25, 1839, Talbot appeared before the Royal Society in person. He read a brief paper entitled "Some account of the art of Photogenic Drawing." The paper described the basics of his picture-making process. Less than a month later, Talbot appeared before the Royal Society to discuss his breakthrough in greater depth.

Talbot made photogenic drawings of simple scenes such as this one, entitled Open Door, *by placing small cameras around his home, Lacock Abbey. Talbot's wife referred to her husband's tiny, wooden cameras as "mousetraps."*

Talbot's Negative-Positive Process

One detail Talbot mentioned was very important. It had to do with a finding he had first noted in 1835. He wrote at the time: "In the Photogenic...process, if the paper is transparent, the first drawing may serve as an object to produce a second drawing, in which the lights and shadows would be reversed."

Talbot's negative-positive process allowed him to make unlimited prints from a single negative. This photo was developed with this process.

The image Talbot captured on the paper in the camera did not look at all like the scene outside. The bright areas of the actual scene appeared dark on the paper, while the dark areas appeared light. Talbot's friend Sir John Herschel later suggested that such an image be called a negative image, or simply a negative.

Talbot reasoned that if he placed a negative on top of a second sheet of sensitized paper and exposed both to sunlight, the process would repeat itself. This time, the bright areas of the original scene would appear light, and shadows would appear dark. As a result, the image on the paper would look just like the actual scene. Herschel suggested that such a likeness be called a positive.

With the negative-positive process, as Talbot's method became known, there was no limit to the number of copies that could be made from a single negative. With Daguerre's process, on the other hand, each daguerreotype was unique. To make a copy of a daguerreotype, the original plate had to be photographed again. Because of the ease of making copies with negatives, Talbot's process was destined to become the most widely used method of photography in the world. Within twelve years, the daguerreotype was nearly obsolete, replaced by various forms of negative-positive photography.

The man who addressed the members of the Royal Society in January and February 1839 believed himself to be a failure. He had wanted to be the first person to invent a new art that would change the world. Although Talbot did not realize it at the time, that was exactly what he had done.

A New Industry

As soon as the world grasped what Daguerre and Talbot had made possible, thousands of people wanted to try taking photographs themselves. Most were free to do so because both Daguerre and Talbot allowed wide use of their discoveries.

Seven months after Daguerre announced that he had devised a method of photography, the French government offered the inventor a lifetime pension for his work. In exchange for the payment, Daguerre agreed to tell the French public all he knew about the photographic process. On August 19, 1839, Daguerre presented his findings to the world.

After Daguerre disclosed details about his process, people in nearly all countries enjoyed the free use of his methods. The only exception was in England. According to his agreement with the French government, Daguerre was allowed to patent his invention outside of France. Expecting that the British, among the wealthiest of the world's peoples, would make wide use of his invention, Daguerre obtained a patent limiting the use of his methods in England.

W. H. Fox Talbot also patented his process in England. The patent required professional photographers to pay Talbot a fee for the right to use his method. Talbot allowed amateur photographers free use of his process, however.

Popularity of Daguerreotypes

At first, most professional photographers preferred Daguerre's method to Talbot's. The issue was not really patent fees; it was the quality of the images each process produced. Daguerreotypes were much clearer than photogenic drawings, or calotypes, as Talbot also called his process, from the Greek words *kalos,* meaning "beautiful," and *typos,* meaning "image."

The problem with Talbot's method was the substance he used to make his

Talbot's calotype process produces soft-edged images that look as though they have been sketched with charcoal.

negatives: writing paper. Made of wood pulp and mashed cloth, writing paper contains countless opaque fibers. Whenever Talbot made a print from a paper negative, the fibers in the negative kept some light from reaching the print paper. As a result, the prints made from paper negatives appeared fuzzy.

Sometimes the soft outlines in Talbot's pictures were quite pleasing, as if the images had been sketched with charcoal. His 1842 portrait entitled *The Chess Players* is a beautiful example of the soft-edged look Talbot's method produced. Most paying customers, however, wanted the clearest possible pictures of themselves and their loved ones. As a result, nearly all professional photographers used Daguerre's method.

Another reason for the popularity of daguerreotypes was the ease of obtaining the equipment needed to produce them. Soon after announcing his discovery, Daguerre formed a partnership with a relative, Alphonse Giroux, to produce daguerreotype cameras. Each camera bore a copy of Daguerre's signature as a guarantee of quality and authenticity. By the end of 1839, Giroux was selling as many cameras as he could make. A new industry had sprung up where none had existed before.

Improving the Lens

As interest in photography grew, scientists around the world tried to improve the photographic process. Most hoped that they, like Giroux, would profit from the new industry.

One of the biggest improvements in photographic equipment came in 1840. Josef Max Petzval, a professor of mathematics at the University of Vienna, Austria, realized that the time required to make a daguerreotype could be cut greatly if the lens allowed more light into the camera. Petzval computed the design of a new lens that would permit sixteen times more light to enter the camera than was possible with the lens used by Daguerre. This reduced the time needed to take a photograph to less than one minute.

The Chess Players *is a fine example of Talbot's calotype process. Opaque fibers in Talbot's paper negatives blocked out small amounts of light in the printing process, creating softly outlined scenes of great mood and feeling.*

More than three million daguerreotypes were taken in the United States between 1840 and 1850. Most were portraits, such as the daguerreotype below of the American artist Thomas Eakins and his sister. Important buildings also interested early photographers. At left is a view of the White House taken around 1846.

Boom of the Portrait Industry

The impact of Petzval's lens was most felt in the business of portraiture. The shorter exposure times allowed by Petzval's lens meant that people no longer had to sit still for several minutes to have their pictures taken. As a result, people began to flock to the new portrait studios. With more customers, photographers could afford to lower their prices. This brought in even more customers. In the decade between 1840 and 1850, more than three million daguerreotypes were taken in the United States alone.

The boom in the portrait business increased the demand for photographic supplies. Photographers needed more chemicals, more photographic plates, and more frames and cases for their finished daguerreotypes. Chemical, glass, and metal manufacturers started new ventures to satisfy these demands. Photographers also needed equipment for their studios: curtains, special chairs, and stands for their cameras. Companies were formed just to provide photographers with what they needed. The sudden growth of the photographic industry created new jobs and new wealth.

Although the daguerreotype's crisp, clear images were popular with professional photographers, the process had its drawbacks. The polished metal surface had to be viewed from just the right angle for the image to be seen. Viewed from the left side, the image appeared in full detail. But viewed from the right side, it appeared half positive and half negative. Viewed from the front, the whole image appeared negative. Because of its limited viewing angles, daguerreotypes were rarely hung on a wall for viewing.

Even when they viewed the daguerreotype from the proper angle, some people found that it produced "a glare offensive to the eye," as the British journal *The Penny Cyclopedia* put it. What was needed was a process that produced something between the sharp, sterile likeness of the daguerreotype and the soft, fuzzy image of the calotype. In 1847, a cousin of Joseph Nicéphore Niépce found the answer.

Glass-Plate Photography

An officer in the French army, Claude Félix Abel Niepce de St. Victor shared his famous cousin's love of science and photography. He realized that Talbot's negative-positive process offered the most practical method of making extra copies of a single photograph. The muted tones of the paper print also appealed to Niepce de St. Victor. He resolved to find a way to improve the process so it would produce clearer pictures.

What was needed was a negative that would allow light to pass through it freely. The material had to remain unchanged by the light-sensitive chemicals placed on it to record the image. It also had to withstand the chemical bath used to fix the image. For Niepce de St. Victor, the answer was obvious. The ideal material was glass.

The problem Niepce de St. Victor faced was how to make the light-sensitive chemicals stick to the glass. Unlike paper, glass did not absorb the solution containing the light-sensitive chemicals, known as the emulsion. Niepce de St. Victor had to find an emulsion that would adhere to the glass without blocking out light. He decided to try egg whites.

Niepce de St. Victor whipped the egg whites until they were stiff, as if he was making a soufflé. He spread the sticky foam onto a glass plate and allowed it to dry. He then dunked the plate into a bath that contained silver nitrate to make the surface sensitive to light.

Niepce de St. Victor's recipe, known as albumen emulsion, worked beautifully. The chemicals on the plate recorded a very clear image. Once the negative image was fixed onto the glass plate, a positive print, known as an albumen print, could be made on paper without any distortion or lost light. The result was an image rich in detail yet muted in tone. The modern photograph was born.

In 1851, glass-plate photography was further refined by Frederick Scott Archer, an English sculptor and photographer. Instead of coating his plates with albumen emulsion, Archer used a clear liquid known as collodion. A mixture of cellulose nitrate, ether, and alcohol, collodion was easier to mix and to store than egg whites were. Once sensitized with silver nitrate, the syrupy mixture was also more sensitive to light than albumen emulsion. As the collodion mixture dried, however, it became less sensitive to light. As a result, Archer learned to use his plates while the emulsion was still wet. For this reason, his method became known as wet-plate photography.

A wet collodion plate could record an image after being exposed for just two seconds. This was the fastest process yet devised. Because of its speed, the quality of the image it produced, and its ability to print unlimited copies, wet-plate photography soon replaced both the daguerreotype and the calotype in photographic studios around the world.

As they became skilled at using the faster, wet-plate method, a few photographers ventured outside their studios to record what they saw and felt. They were about to change forever the way people would view the world and themselves.

A Visual Record

Before the invention of photography, people learned about the appearance of distant landscapes, wildlife, people, and events mainly through the work of artists. Hand-drawn portraits printed on stamps and paper money revealed what kings, queens, presidents, and prime ministers looked like. Woodcuts and engravings printed in newspapers and books portrayed other important people and events. When naturalists ventured into the wilderness to discover new species, they took along pencils and paint to record their findings.

The American writer Edgar Allan Poe wrote that the photograph revealed "a more absolute truth than the work of ordinary art."

Teaching About the World

Photography changed all that. Slowly, photographs replaced paintings and drawings as the main way people learned about the appearance of the world beyond the one in which they lived. Artists continued to paint, draw, and sculpt, but few devoted themselves to the task of documenting the physical world. That job passed to the photographer.

People valued photographs because they seemed to offer a sense of realness that drawings lacked. When people viewed a drawing, they knew they were not seeing the subject itself, but an artist's view of the subject. With a photograph, however, people felt they were looking upon the subject itself, as though viewing it through a magic telescope.

The realness of the photograph comes from the very process of making it. As W. H. Fox Talbot put it, the photograph is created "by the agency of Light alone, without any aid whatever from the artist's pencil." Because the photographic image is formed directly from the subject, not through the eye and hand of the artist, the American writer Edgar Allan Poe said it reveals "a more absolute truth than the work of ordinary art."

The camera is also a physical witness to the moment it records. An artist can be thousands of miles away from his or her subject and still create its likeness. The camera cannot. It must be in the presence of the subject when the image is recorded.

A Bond with Reality

For some people, knowledge about the chemical process of recording an image adds to the realness of the photograph. These people realize that it is light reflected from the subject of the photograph that alters the chemicals on the surface of the photographic plate. This physical change, they feel, creates a sort of bond between the subject and the plate. The British poet Elizabeth Barrett described such feelings about the photographic process in a letter she wrote in 1843:

> It is not merely the likeness which is precious in such cases—but the association and the sense of nearness involved in the thing...the fact of the *very shadow of the person* lying there fixed forever!...I would rather have such a memorial of one I dearly loved, than the noblest artist's work ever produced.

People continue to believe in the realness of photographs today. Although photographers have learned to alter images in many ways, a photograph is still considered a true likeness of a thing or an event. For this reason, photographs can be used as evidence in trials.

The realness of the photograph also has to do with the time it takes to record an image. Before photography, artists were often hired to sketch an important event so they could later depict it in a painting or drawing. Glancing from one figure to another, the artist would try to capture the posture and gestures of each person present. Later, the artist would fill in missing details. With a photograph, there is no need to blend moments together or to fill in missing details later. The camera sees everything—all at once—and preserves it forever.

Capturing Moments in Time

The camera's ability to capture a single moment in time appealed to those who wanted to record history as it happened. Not long after Daguerre revealed his discovery to the world, French officials hired a photographer to record the opening of a railway connecting France and Belgium. Photographers also were hired to record coronations, important speeches, and the signings of treaties between nations.

With photography, people were able to record an important event as it happened, with no need to fill in missing details later. The camera saw everything—all at once—and preserved it forever.

Events were not the only subjects photographers tried to capture before they slipped into the past. For example, the government of France hired photographers in 1851 to make a lasting record of important French buildings, including the palace at Versailles.

"The Eye of History"

An American photographer named Mathew B. Brady believed that people of great importance also should be photographed. "The camera is the eye of history," Brady wrote. "From the very first I regarded myself as under obligation to my country to preserve the faces of its historic men and mothers."

Beginning in 1844, Brady set out to photograph "the most eminent citizens of the American Republic since the days of Washington." His subjects included Henry Clay, Daniel Webster, John James Audubon, and others. In 1850, Brady published a collection of his work entitled *The Gallery of Illustrious Americans*. The five-pound book cost thirty dollars, a huge sum of money in 1850.

Photographs in Politics

In 1860, Brady photographed Abraham Lincoln when the candidate for president visited New York City to give a speech at Cooper Union College. Brady's portrait revealed a calm, earnest, and honest-looking human being. Thousands of copies of Brady's photograph were circulated by Lincoln's admirers.

After his election in 1860, Lincoln said, "Brady and the Cooper Union

Mathew B. Brady, photographed in his own studio with two of his relatives (top), called the camera "the eye of history." His 1860 portrait of Abraham Lincoln (bottom), helped the congressman from Illinois become better known in the eastern United States.

speech made me president." The president was exaggerating, but his comment contained more than a little truth. Ever since Lincoln, candidates for president have taken great care to have their pictures taken and circulated.

The impact of Brady's photography on the nation did not end with Lincoln's election; it began with it. Shortly after Lincoln's inauguration in 1861, seven southern states declared their independence from the United States of America. Lincoln responded by ordering his army to put down the rebellion. This was the beginning of the American Civil War, one of the first wars to be photographed. The man behind most of these photographs was Mathew B. Brady.

When the war broke out, Brady owned three of the largest photography studios in the United States—two in New York City and one in Washington, D.C. Thousands of soldiers on their way to battle stopped into Brady's studios to have their photographs taken. These haunting portraits show how young, serious, and nervous many of the soldiers were.

Brady did not limit his record of the war to the faces of the young men who stopped into his studio. Soon after the

With the personal backing of President Lincoln, Mathew Brady and his assistants ventured onto the battlefields and into the camps to photograph the American Civil War. (Above) A Confederate soldier lies dead. (Below) Union troops assemble at camp.

Brady and his assistants outfitted wagons with darkroom equipment and took them onto the battlefield in order to prepare and develop wet-plate negatives. The Union troops nicknamed the odd-looking wagons the "Whatsits."

war broke out, Brady asked President Lincoln for permission to follow the Union army into battle. The president responded by writing something on a small piece of paper then handing the note to Brady. The message consisted of just two words: "Pass Brady." Beneath the order was Lincoln's signature. With Lincoln's personal backing, Brady and his assistants ventured onto the battlefields of the Civil War to take some of the most memorable war photographs of all time.

Photographing the Civil War

Brady outfitted horse-drawn wagons with small darkrooms for making and developing the wet-plate negatives. When members of the Union army first saw one of these wagons, they thought it looked quite odd. "What is it?" the soldiers asked. "It's a Whatsit!" they joked. Loaded with chemicals and fragile glass plates, twenty-two of Brady's "Whatsit" wagons trundled along back roads and through fields to record the details of the bloody conflict.

The wet-plate process Brady used required exposures from five to ten seconds in length. This was too slow to capture the action of battle, so Brady

and his assistants concentrated on recording the gruesome aftermath of the fighting.

Their photographs made the horror of war apparent to all. In one photograph, a Union soldier lies face down on a muddy road, his body ripped by bullets. In another, a Confederate officer rests on his back in a grassy field. A few feet away lies his severed arm. In the background of almost every photograph is the same thing: bodies as far as the camera's eye could see. At such a distance, it is impossible to tell for which side the soldiers fought.

Brady's photographs were shown in his studios in New York City and Washington, D.C. "Mr. Brady has done something to bring home to us the terrible reality and earnestness of the war," wrote the reporter for one newspaper. "Crowds of people are constantly going up the stairs," the reporter continued, describing the scene in the gallery. "Follow them and you will find them bending over photographic views of the fearful battlefield, taken immediately after the action."

At the time, the pictures were too grim for many people to bear. Describing the reaction to photographs taken after the battle of Antietam in 1862, the famous American author Oliver Wendell Holmes wrote:

The field of photography is extending itself to embrace the subjects of strange and sometimes fearful interest.... We have now before us a series of photographs showing the field of Antietam.... Let him who wishes to know what the war is look at this series of illustrations. These wrecks of manhood thrown together in careless heaps or ranged in ghastly rows for burial were alive but yesterday.... Many people would not look through this series. Many, having seen it and dreamed of its horrors, would lock it up in some secret drawer.

Even after the war, many people did not care to view Brady's pictures. Brady had spent $100,000 of his own money to take more than seven thousand photographs of the Civil War. He sold prints of these photographs for just twenty-five cents, but few people bought them. Brady offered his negatives to the National Archives, but the government was not interested. Brady had to close his New York galleries and sell much of his equipment to pay his bills. He gave one set of Civil War negatives to pay off a creditor. Finally in 1875, the U.S. Congress purchased what remained of Brady's collection.

In the years since, Brady's photographs have been exhibited at major museums and have appeared in countless books about the Civil War, creating a visual impression of the war for hundreds of millions of people around the world. In 1990, the filmmaker Ken Burns made

After the Civil War, one of Brady's assistants, Timothy O'Sullivan, traveled to the American West as the official photographer of the 40th Parallel Survey. While on the journey, O'Sullivan took this striking photograph of the Shoshone Falls on the Snake River in Idaho.

Timothy O'Sullivan's most famous photograph is this image of the cliff dwelling in Canyon de Chelly, Arizona. O'Sullivan took the picture while serving as the photographer for the Army Corps of Engineers.

a documentary about the Civil War that was the most-watched program in the history of American public television. Many of the images that appeared on the screen during the eleven-hour program were photographs taken by Mathew B. Brady and his assistants.

After the war, America's photographers turned their attention to other things. Brady himself returned to the portrait business. One of Brady's most talented assistants, Timothy O'Sullivan, journeyed westward.

Photography Travels West

In 1867, O'Sullivan was hired by the U.S. government as the official photographer of the 40th Parallel Survey. The mission of the survey party was to explore a nine-hundred-mile stretch of land between

Virginia City, Nevada, and Denver, Colorado, along the 40th Parallel. The 40th Parallel is the imaginary line that encircles the earth parallel to the equator at the fortieth degree of latitude north, about 2,750 miles north of the equator. "It is the object of the Government to ascertain all the characteristics of the region," states the survey report. "The minerals, the flora and the fauna of the country are likewise to be studied and reported on. In fact, all the work of nature in that wild and unknown region is to be scanned by shrewd and highly educated observers."

No one in the survey party proved to be a more careful observer than O'Sullivan. Using a lighting device of his own design, O'Sullivan took flash pictures deep within the tunnels of the Comstock lode mine. He lugged heavy equipment high into the mountains to

William Henry Jackson took many photographs of pioneers exploring the American West.

capture panoramas of unspoiled beauty. Crossing rivers and deserts at great risk, O'Sullivan recorded one monumental scene after another.

The 40th Parallel Survey ended in 1869. In 1871, O'Sullivan returned to the West as a photographer for the Army Corps of Engineers. O'Sullivan and the corps traveled through Nevada, Utah, Arizona, and New Mexico. On this journey, O'Sullivan took what was to become his most famous photograph, a beautifully composed view of the ancient cliff dwellings in Canyon de Chelly, Arizona. O'Sullivan also photographed members of the Zuni and Magia tribes who lived in the area.

Yellowstone

O'Sullivan was not the only person to achieve fame by photographing the West. A photographer named Willam Henry Jackson accompanied a U.S. government survey party to a remote area of Wyoming known for its unusual beauty. Jackson took nearly four hundred photographs of giant geysers, hot springs, and waterfalls, as well as a vast, colorful canyon known as Yellowstone.

Stories about Yellowstone had convinced Senator S. C. Pomeroy of Kansas that the area should be protected by law, so in 1871 he introduced a bill to preserve the land. Pomeroy's bill did not advance very far. Few members of Congress believed what Pomeroy told them about the area. When Pomeroy heard about Jackson's visit to Yellowstone, he told his colleagues, "There are photographs of the valley and of the curiosities, which the senators can see." Pomeroy arranged to have Jackson's photographs brought before Congress.

After seeing Jackson's photographs, the members of Congress quickly passed Pomeroy's bill. On March 1, 1872, President Ulysses S. Grant signed the bill into law, making Yellowstone the nation's first national park.

Pictures in Stereo

Jackson continued to tour the West, taking pictures of the Grand Canyon, Bryce Canyon, and many other natural wonders. Many of his most popular pictures were taken with a special device known as a stereoscopic camera.

This device was designed to mimic the workings of human vision. It contained two separate cameras with lenses set about two and a half inches apart—the average distance between a person's eyes. When the photographer pressed a button, both cameras took a picture at the same time, recording two slightly different views of the same subject. The negatives were later printed side by side on a card known as a stereograph. When a person looked at the stereograph through a viewing device called a stereoscope, the side-by-side images formed a single three-dimensional image in the person's mind.

Stereoscopes became very popular. American companies like Keystone, Underwood and Underwood, and E. & H. T. Anthony sold thousands of stereoscopes and millions of photographs to go with them. But they soon needed more.

Photographers scoured the globe in search of new subjects. From the palaces of Europe to the pyramids of Egypt, from the deserts of Africa to the mountains of Tibet, photographers cataloged the wonders of the world. They rode in hot-air balloons to photograph the land from above. They boarded ships to record views from the sea. They visited great cities and unknown villages to record the diversity of people around the world. People had an insatiable interest in purchasing and collecting these photos.

The lives of ordinary people were transformed by photography. "For an absurdly small sum, we may become familiar not only with every famous locality in the world, but also with almost every man of note in Europe," wrote a columnist in 1861 for *Once a Week,* a journal published in London.

> All of us have seen the Alps and know Chamonix and the Mer de Glace by heart, though we have never braved the horrors of the Channel....We have crossed the Andes, ascended Tenerife, entered Japan, "done" Niagara and the Thousand Isles, drunk [the] delight of the battle with our peers (at shop windows), sat at the councils of the mighty, grown familiar with kings, emperors, queens, prima donnas, pets of the ballet, and "well graced actors." Ghosts we have seen and have not trembled; stood before royalty and have not uncovered; and looked, in short, through a three-inch lens at every single pomp and vanity of this wicked but beautiful world.

The changes brought about by photography between 1839 and 1879 were nothing short of revolutionary. Suddenly, nearly everyone and everything in the wide world could be viewed with ease. But the photographic revolution had scarcely begun.

A New Form of News

On Tuesday, December 2, 1873, the *Daily Graphic,* a New York City newspaper, published a picture of a building known as Steinway Hall. This was not unusual. Pictures had appeared in newspapers for nearly three centuries. But there was something very different and very important about this picture. It was a photograph.

When Joseph Nicéphore Niépce began to experiment with the photographic process in 1820, his goal was to find a practical method of printing images on paper. He succeeded in 1822 with the process he called heliogravure, but Niépce's findings led him away from printing and into a whole new art, photography.

Getting Pictures into Newspapers

Nearly twenty years passed before printing and photography again were joined. When they were, it was with a process similar to heliogravure that was developed by W. H. Fox Talbot in 1852. Talbot coated a glass plate with a light-sensitive gelatin that turned hard when exposed to light. Talbot then placed a piece of gauze between the source of light and the plate. The gauze screen broke the light into a fine pattern of dots. Exposed to light, the chemicals within each dot either turned hard or remained soft. Talbot washed the soft gelatins away with hot water, leaving a pattern of dots from which to print. Where dots were clustered together, the image appeared black or dark gray. Where they were spaced farther apart, the image appeared light gray or white. Because this process reproduced images with dots rather than with solid tones, it became known as the halftone process. The images produced using this method are known as halftones.

Since the chemicals used to create halftones did not have to respond to fine shadings of gray, later printers were able to coat their plates with chemicals that were cheaper to produce than the fine gelatins Talbot used. After more than twenty years, the halftone process became affordable for newspapers or magazines. Once it did, it changed news reporting forever.

The Birth of Photojournalism

When word about the breakthrough at the *Daily Graphic* reached other newspapers, editors around the world decided to print photographs in their papers as well. They needed photographs—many of them—of a whole new kind. They wanted photographs that illustrated news stories, or, even better, told stories themselves. A whole new form of photography was born, a form which later came to be known as photojournalism.

Photographers took to the streets to give the editors what they wanted. They

Finding wet-plate photography clumsy and difficult, a bank clerk named George Eastman created simple, easy-to-handle photographic negatives.

rushed to the scenes of crimes, fires, and natural disasters to record what had happened. They photographed powerful people as they shaped events and the unknown people whose lives were changed by them.

Not long after the editor of the *Daily Graphic* published the first newspaper photograph, another New Yorker began to work on a device that would give photographers even greater freedom to pursue the news. In 1880, a bank clerk named George Eastman built a machine that could produce a new kind of photographic plate: the dry plate.

Dry Plates and Strip Film

Eastman's dry plates were pieces of glass coated with a mixture of gelatin and silver bromide. Unlike collodion, the dry-plate emulsion did not lose its sensitivity to light with time. As a result, a photographer could buy a pack of dry plates and use them whenever he or she wanted to. Since the plates were precoated with emulsion, the news photographer did not need to haul around a portable darkroom in which to sensitize the plates, as was the practice with wet plates. The biggest advantage of the dry plates, however, was the shorter exposure time they required. Dry plates became fully exposed ten times faster than wet plates did. Exposure times were cut from a few seconds to a few tenths of one second.

As soon as Eastman perfected the dry plate, he began work on an even better material on which to "draw with light." He called his invention American Film. Introduced in 1884, Eastman's film was a strip of paper coated with a thin, clear gelatin emulsion. The film was stored on rollers inside the camera. After an exposure was made, the photographer turned the rollers to expose a new portion of film. Each roll of film had room for dozens of pictures. After the entire roll was exposed and developed, the photographer peeled away the paper backing, leaving a strip of negatives from which to make positive prints.

Photography Changes Society

With the coming of dry plates and roll film, photographers were able to take a new kind of photograph—the unposed or candid photograph. One of the first photographers to take advantage of the faster exposure times these materials offered was Jacob A. Riis. A reporter for the New York *Evening Sun,* Riis often illustrated his written stories with his own photographs. In the 1890s, Riis took his camera into the slums of New York City to record the anguish of the people living there. He had to work quickly, since few of his subjects cared

ROLL FILM

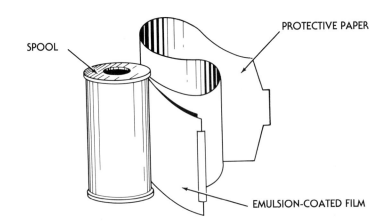

SPOOL

PROTECTIVE PAPER

EMULSION-COATED FILM

In 1884 George Eastman's invention of roll film, or American Film as he called it, freed photographers from the cumbersome process of inserting a glass plate into the camera for every exposure. It made photography faster, more convenient, and more affordable, and it led to the development of small, portable cameras.

Roll film consisted of a strip of celluloid that was coated with an emulsion containing light-sensitive silver nitrate.

The film was backed with light-proof paper that protected it from exposure to any light except from the camera's shutter. Stored on a spool that fit inside the camera, the film was turned to expose a new section after each exposure. A single roll of this film could be used to take dozens of pictures. After the film was developed and fixed, the paper backing was peeled off, leaving a strip of negatives from which positive prints were made.

to be photographed. Sometimes his subjects were not only camera shy, but also downright hostile. He wrote, "Yet even from Hell's Kitchen had I not long before been driven forth with my camera by a band of angry women who pelted me with brickbats and stones on my retreat, shouting at me never to come back."

Despite the difficulties he faced, Riis was able to gracefully depict the grim world hidden within America's richest city. One photograph reveals a band of homeless men huddled under a porch, sharing a meal from a tin can. Another captures a group of lodgers crammed together in a "five-cent-a-spot" flophouse

A reporter for the New York Evening Sun, *Jacob A. Riis often illustrated his written stories with photographs.*

Riis's studies of life in the slums of New York City caused an uproar that led to important reforms. (Left) Homeless men share a can of food. (Below right) Lodgers crowd into a room on Bayard Street.

(Above left) Two boys dressed in rags pose for a portrait. (Right) A child laborer works in a garment shop.

Riis revealed a grim world hidden within New York City, America's richest city. (Right) Rough characters stare at the camera in a photograph entitled Bandit's Roost. In a dramatic photograph titled Street Arabs (below), Riis revealed the pathetic condition of children living in New York slums.

on Bayard Street. In one of his most touching photographs, *Street Arabs*, Riis shows three shoeless children dozing beside a sidewalk grate.

Riis's photographs shocked the people of New York. Thousands of concerned citizens demanded that the government do something about the poverty depicted in them. Under pressure, the leaders of New York agreed to take action. Several of the buildings Riis photographed were condemned as un-safe and torn down. The power of the photograph was proved once again.

At the same time Riis was portraying the plight of immigrants living in slums on the East Coast of the United States, a photographer named Arnold Genthe was photographing immigrants on the West Coast.

An artist from Germany, Genthe was intrigued by the thousands of Chinese immigrants living within a twelve-square-block section of San Francisco known as Chinatown. At first, Genthe tried to sketch scenes from life in Chinatown, but the immigrants objected. They believed that if a person owned the likeness of someone else, the person with the picture could work sorcery on the other person. Despite the misgivings of his subjects, Genthe persisted. He bought a compact camera, loaded it with film, and concealed it within his clothing. He then ventured into Chinatown. When he happened upon a striking scene, Genthe took out his camera and snapped a picture. Even at the speed he worked, Genthe was able to produce beautifully composed photographs of great artistic and historical value.

Arnold Genthe recorded the destruction caused by the earthquake that struck San Francisco on April 18, 1906. (Left) Smoke rises from the rubble of collapsed buildings.

A Great Disaster

Genthe would have been satisfied to be known simply for his Chinatown photographs, but fate decided otherwise. At 5:12 on the morning of Wednesday, April 18, 1906, shock waves from the most powerful earthquake ever to strike California ripped through San Francisco. Chimneys toppled. Walls collapsed. Houses twisted off their foundations. A news editor for the San Francisco *Examiner* named John Barret wrote, "Trolley tracks were twisted, their wires down, wriggling like serpents, flashing blue sparks all the time."

Genthe and thousands of others fled their homes. Genthe's own camera was destroyed, but he borrowed another. As the dawn lit the city, Genthe began to record the disaster. He took pictures of

ruined buildings, damaged streets, and stricken survivors. By noon, large fires burned throughout the city. Climbing to the heights of the city's many hills,

(Left) Genthe's photograph shows houses ripped from their foundations by the most powerful earthquake known to have struck California. (Above) The facade and rear wall of a building still stand after the roof and side walls have collapsed.

(Right) A photograph by Dorothea Lange depicts the plight of an eighteen-year-old mother from Oklahoma who was left stranded and penniless in a migrant camp in the Imperial Valley of California during the Great Depression. (Below) Robert Capa's image of a soldier killed during the Spanish Civil War remains one of the most disturbing war photographs ever taken.

Genthe photographed clouds of smoke billowing over the wrecked buildings. One of Genthe's photographs, a view down Sacramento Street, is one of the most memorable news photographs of all time.

Recording News as It Happens

The increased speed of cameras and film allowed news photographers to capture events as they unfolded, freezing the action. In 1910, a photographer was taking a picture of the mayor of New York, William Gaynor, just as an assassin attacked. The photograph showed the mayor collapsing immediately after being shot.

The new, faster film meant that war photographers could record not just the aftermath of battles, but the fighting itself. When the Spanish-American War broke out in 1912, a photographer named James Hare was able to send home compelling images of fierce fighting. In the Spanish Civil War in 1936, a photographer named Robert Capa snapped an incredible picture of a Spanish soldier at the very moment he was struck by machine-gun fire. The gruesome image remains one of the most disturbing war photographs ever taken.

Photography in the Great Depression

While Capa was covering the war in Spain, photojournalists in the United States were busy documenting the hardships caused by the Great Depression.

Dorothea Lange's photographs of life in a California migrant camp were taken as part of the Farm Security Administration (FSA) project to document the Depression. (Left) A man and his family pose outside a trailer.

During this financial calamity, millions of Americans lost their jobs. At the same time, one of the worst droughts in American history turned much of the Midwest into a windblown desert known as the Dust Bowl. Pictures of closed factories, locked banks, long soup lines, and devastated farms appeared in newspapers across the country.

To provide out-of-work photographers with jobs, an agency of the federal government known as the Farm Security Administration (FSA) hired photographers to travel around the country, documenting what they saw. The goal of the program was to portray the inner strength of rural Americans as they coped with difficulties of the time. To realize this vision, the director of the project, Roy Stryker, recruited the most

Lange's portrait of a mother with her two children (above), was judged by the editors of Time *magazine to be one of the ten greatest news photographs ever taken. (Left) While working for the FSA in 1936, Arthur Rothstein took this unforgettable picture of a family seeking shelter from a dust storm in Oklahoma.*

gifted photographers of the era, including Dorothea Lange, Gordon Parks, Walker Evans, and Marion Post Walcott. The 270,000 photographs taken by these and other photographers remain a monument to the spirit of the American people—and to the genius of the photographic artists who captured it on film.

At the same time the FSA photographers were recording how Americans coped with the depression, twenty-two news photographers were on hand to witness one of the most spectacular disasters of modern history. On May 6, 1937, the dirigible *Hindenburg* approached the airfield in Lakehurst, New Jersey, to land after having crossed the

(Above right) In 1936, Henry Luce, publisher of Time *and* Fortune *magazines, introduced a photographic magazine called* Life. *Photographers for the magazine pioneered a new form of photojournalism: the photo essay. (Below) The explosion of the dirigible* Hindenburg *on May 6, 1937, was photographed by at least twenty-two news photographers.*

Atlantic Ocean. On the ground, a crowd of spectators watched as the great airship maneuvered above them. Suddenly, the rear quarter of the ship exploded into a giant fireball. Within seconds, flames engulfed the passenger compartment, instantly killing all one hundred passengers and crew. Below, the horrified photographers recorded it all.

"To See Life"

Not all great news photographs were tragic, of course. Newly elected presidents, historic meetings, successful feats of exploration, and even thrilling sports events appeared in the pages of newspapers around the world. Photojournalism became so popular that Henry Luce, the publisher of *Time* and *Fortune* magazines, decided to publish a magazine that would consist entirely of photographs and captions. In 1936, the first issue of *Life* magazine appeared. Introducing it, Luce described not only the purpose of his publication, but also the very essence of photojournalism itself:

> To see life, to see the world, to eyewitness great events; to watch the faces of the poor and the gestures of the proud; to see strange things—machines, armies, multitudes, shadows in the jungle and on the moon; to see man's work—his paintings, towers, and discoveries; to see things a thousand miles away, things hidden behind walls and within rooms, things dangerous to come to...to see and take pleasure in seeing; to see and be amazed; to see and be instructed.

Beginning with its first issue, *Life* pioneered a form of photojournalism that has become a staple of the print

One of Life *magazine's most talented photographers, Gordon Parks, took this picture of a black cleaning lady in Washington, D.C., in 1942.*

media: the photo essay. A photo essay tells an entire news story with just pictures and captions. The *Life* photographers like Gordon Parks, Alfred Eisenstadt, and Margaret Bourke-White were assigned to shoot photo essays across the country and around the globe.

Bourke-White contributed some of *Life*'s most memorable photographs, beginning with a picture of the Fort Peck Dam in Montana that graced the cover of the very first issue. The first woman photographer assigned to U.S. military operations, Bourke-White flew on combat missions during World War II and traveled with ground troops as they battled Nazi forces across Europe. Arriving at the Buchenwald concentration camp within hours of the German retreat, Bourke-White took the most haunting picture of her career: a stark black-and-white image of the Jewish prisoners awaiting their liberation.

Capturing Unforgettable Instants

Although motion pictures and television have joined still photography in the coverage of the news, photojournalism remains as important today as ever. Perhaps the reason lies in the very stillness of the image. The viewer of a photograph is able to focus on details of an event without the distractions of motion.

For example, on November 24, 1963, millions of Americans watched on television as a nightclub owner named Jack Ruby stepped from the shadows of the Dallas city jail and shot Lee Harvey Oswald, the accused assassin of President John F. Kennedy. A videotape of the event was played countless times on news programs over the next few days. But for many people, a still photograph by Bob Jackson of the Dallas *Times Herald* taken during Ruby's attack creates an even more vivid impression of the historic event than the live footage does.

Like the videotape, Jackson's Pulitzer-prizewinning photo captures the anguish on Oswald's face as the accused killer crumples in pain. But the photograph shows more—the murderous intent of Ruby as he moves in on his victim and the shock, confusion, and fear on the faces of the police officers who were Oswald's escorts. As the eye travels from one frozen figure to another, reading the emotions in each face, the viewer's imagination re-creates the moment, bringing it alive.

The haunting faces of Buchenwald prisoners were captured in this photograph taken by Margaret Bourke-White at the end of World War II.

Despite competition from television and motion pictures, photographs remain one of the most powerful ways to record news events. Huynh Cong Ut's image of children fleeing down Route 1 near Trang Bang captured the horror of the Vietnam War.

Bringing War Home

The enduring importance of still photographs was reaffirmed during the Vietnam War later in the 1960s. Television cameras brought the war into nearly every home in America, but it was a handful of remarkable photographs that stirred the greatest passions. Malcolm Brown's picture of the self-immolation of Quang Duc, Eddie Adams's photo of the execution of a Viet Cong prisoner, and Huynh Cong Ut's image of children fleeing down Route 1 near Trang Bang stirred deep feelings in almost all who saw them. The images have lost none of their power. They remain grim reminders of the horrors of the war.

The war in the Persian Gulf brought Americans a new kind of video reporting—straight from television cameras mounted in the weapons themselves. But it was still photographs of wounded

Malcolm Brown's picture of the self-immolation of Quang Duc stirred the consciences of people around the world.

David Turnley of the Detroit Free Press *captured the human cost of the Persian Gulf War with this image of Sgt. Ken Kozakiewicz reacting to the death of his friend.*

American soldiers, civilian refugees fleeing from Baghdad, and the jubilant Kuwaitis returning to their homeland that gave the war a human face.

One of the most dramatic pictures of the war was taken by David Turnley of the *Detroit Free Press*. Traveling with a medical unit by helicopter, Turnley watched as U.S. ground troops pulled injured American soldiers from a Bradley armored vehicle. One of the soldiers, Sgt. Ken Kozakiewicz, had a fractured hand. Turnley photographed the soldier as he was being helped toward the helicopter. The driver of the vehicle, who was Kozakiewicz's friend, was dead. Turnley wrote:

The medical staff collected the body of the Bradley driver in a bag, put it on the chopper, and handed the driver's identification card to Kozakiewicz. It was only then that the sergeant realized the body in the bag was his friend. This was the moment captured in the photograph.

If history is any guide, Turnley's photograph will remain in the world's memory long after the bomb's-eye-view videotapes are forgotten.

CHAPTER 7

Photography Comes Home

The world's first photographs were taken in the home. Joseph Nicéphore Niépce placed a camera in the window of his home, Maison Gras, in Saint-Loup-de-Varennes, France, to take the world's first photograph, a view of his courtyard. W. H. Fox Talbot developed his negative-positive process by placing his "mousetraps" around Lacock Abbey in Wiltshire, England, photographing such things as a latticed window, shelves of glassware and china, and a broom propped up beside an open door. Onc of Louis Daguerre's oldest surviving photographs is a still life of a set table.

Once the invention of photography became widely known, however, most of those who practiced the new art did so outside the home. Almost all of the early photographers were professionals. Photographic equipment was expensive, and the process of preparing and developing photographic plates was complicated. Few amateurs had the time or money to dabble in photography.

Most professional photographers worked in studios, taking portraits. Some traveled around the world, searching for new and exotic subjects to photograph. A few early photographers took pictures of their home life, but such pictures are rare.

The Home Camera

All that changed in 1888. In June of that year, George Eastman, the inventor of American Film, began to sell a twenty-five-dollar, handheld camera designed for nonprofessionals. He called it the Kodak.

The Kodak camera, invented by George Eastman, made it easy for amateurs to take pictures, like this one of a cabin in the woods.

THE FIRST KODAK

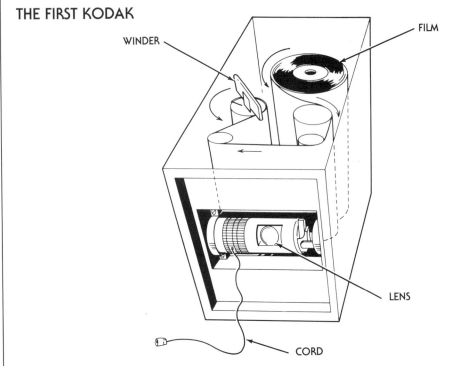

WINDER

FILM

LENS

CORD

George Eastman introduced the first Kodak camera in 1888. The camera was extremely easy to use, and it marked the beginning of home photography. The first Kodak had no viewfinder. The user just pointed the lens toward the scene or subject to be photographed and pulled a cord to release, or open, the shutter. After each exposure, the roll film sealed inside the camera was advanced by turning a key on the top of the camera.

Until the introduction of the Kodak, most cameras were owned by profes-sional photographers. Photographers developed their own film and made their own prints. With the Kodak, the photographer did not even load or un-load the film. When the 100 exposures on the roll film were all taken, the owner mailed the camera to the Eastman Company, where the film was developed, prints were made, and a new roll film was sealed inside the cam-era. This was the beginning of the com-mercial industry of film developing and printing.

The Kodak camera was very easy to use. According to the instruction manu-al, all a person had to do was: "1. Point the camera. 2. Press the button. 3. Turn the key. 4. Pull the cord."

The owner of a Kodak camera never touched the film. The camera was sold with a roll of film sealed inside. The roll contained space for one hundred circu-lar pictures, each two and a half inches wide. Once the roll was exposed, the owner mailed the entire camera plus ten dollars back to the Eastman Com-pany in Rochester, New York.

The Eastman Company employees opened the camera, removed the film, and sealed a new roll of film inside. The workers developed the exposed film and made prints from the negatives. The finished prints, negatives, and loaded camera were then returned to the owner. "You press the button, we do the rest," promised Eastman in his advertising. His slogan was true.

Eastman's camera became an instant success. More than ninety thousand people bought the Kodak camera within the first four years after it was introduced. By the time the first roll of film in these cameras was used, more than nine million photographs had been taken. Soon, Kodak owners were taking more photographs each year than all professional photographers combined.

The photographs taken by amateurs looked different than those taken by professionals. Most amateurs took Eastman at his word. They just pointed the camera and pressed the button.

(Left) The pictures taken with the earliest Kodak cameras were round. (Above) Three young women pose for an early snapshot at the beach.

They lacked the professional's sense of composition—the arrangement of the image within the frame of the photograph—and they were less aware of the effects of light and shadow on the final image.

"The Eye of the Family"

Although the photographs taken by amateurs did not look as well crafted as those taken by professionals, they still held value for those who took them. In fact, most people cared more about their own photographs than any pictures taken by professionals. These snapshots often preserved images of personal meaning—birthdays, anniversaries, graduations, baptisms, and bar mitzvahs. As George Eastman put it, "The Kodak camera makes possible a collection of photographs which record the life of its owner and which increase in value each day that passes."

Parents often use cameras to preserve precious moments in the lives of their children.

Posing for family portraits became commonplace thanks to the ease and affordability of amateur photography.

Mathew Brady called the camera "the eye of history." George Eastman made it the "eye of the family." Each Kodak user became his or her family's Mathew Brady, recording the history of the family and preserving the images of family members. Some parents, grandparents, and great-grandparents are known to their descendants through photographs alone.

Photographs also help people see themselves as others see them. A mirror reverses a person's image. A photograph does not. Photographs can give people views of themselves difficult or impossible to see in a mirror—from the side, from behind, from slightly above or a bit below. These views often help people feel good about how they look. Sometimes, the knowledge gained from photographs inspires people to alter their appearance. After seeing a photograph, a person may decide to change his or her hair style, lose weight, or dress differently.

A Trivial Art?

Many people have had doubts about the kind of knowledge gained from photographs. One of the first people to question the value of photography was the French poet Charles Baudelaire, who lived at the time of Daguerre. Among other things, Baudelaire believed photography led people to become overly concerned with their looks. He compared such people to Narcissus, the boy in Greek mythology who fell in love with

Despite the popularity of home photography, people continued to have professional photographers take formal portraits. Here, a young girl poses to record her confirmation day.

the image of himself reflected in a pool. Describing the invention of the daguerreotype, Baudelaire wrote, "From that moment onwards, our sordid society rushed, Narcissus-like, to gaze at its trivial image on a metal plate."

Other people believe that instead of aiding memory, photography actually impairs it. Trusting the camera to record an event, a person may not bother to form a vivid impression of what is happening. The photograph will show how the event appeared, but it cannot supply the sounds, smells, and feelings that made the moment special. Without memory, say these critics, the richness of an experience is lost.

Other people dislike how the act of taking a picture can disrupt an event. For these people, pausing for a photograph does not preserve a moment, it spoils it. These people are especially annoyed by photographers who interrupt what is going on by shouting, "Smile" or "Look this way."

Despite these drawbacks, home photography continued to grow in popularity in the early twentieth century. As more people took up the hobby, camera manufacturers competed for their business by making cameras that were easier to use, produced better pictures, or both. One of the most important breakthroughs was conceived around 1905 by a German inventor name Oskar Barnack.

The Compact Camera

Tired of lugging around his bulky 5 x 7 view camera, a camera that takes very clear photographs because of its large negatives, Barnack decided to build a compact camera that would produce pictures of equal quality. The head of the new products department of Ernst Leitz, an optical equipment company, Barnack realized that such a dream camera would have to be able to produce a small negative and a large picture.

Barnack built his camera, trimmed the film from his 5 x 7 camera to fit into it, and made a few exposures. The developed negatives looked good, but Barnack was not pleased with the enlarged prints he made from them. Too many details were missing.

The problem was the film Barnack used. The granules of silver in the standard emulsion were too large and too far apart to produce the detail Barnack needed. When the tiny negative was enlarged, the distance between the granules increased, leaving blank spots on the print. As a result, the finished image looked blurry, or grainy. Disappointed, Barnack put his dream camera aside.

Years later, Barnack was in charge of developing a new film for motion picture cameras. As he worked on the project, Barnack began to think of his little camera. The new film contained fine granules of silver, since the small motion picture images had to be projected onto a large screen. Once the new film was finished, Barnack snipped off a length of it and fitted it on rollers inside his small camera. With the new film, Barnack's enlargements came out crisp and clear. The inventor's dream had come true.

Ernst Leitz unveiled Barnack's camera at the Leipzig Fair in 1925. The camera was named the Leica, short for Leitz Camera. It also became known as the 35-millimeter camera, since that was the width of the motion picture film it used.

Clear Pictures with Less Light

The 35-millimeter, or 35mm, camera allowed both amateurs and professionals to take very clear pictures with less light than was needed by larger cameras. The reason is as old as photography itself. W. H. Fox Talbot realized as early as 1835 that film placed close to an aperture will record an image much faster and with less light than will film that is farther away.

When the distance between the lens and the negative, known as the focal length, is short, the light entering the aperture is concentrated on a small portion of the film. The intense light makes a strong impression on the negative. With a longer focal length, the same amount of light is spread across a larger area, making a weaker impression. This is why Talbot built "mousetraps" that were only about two and a half inches long.

Talbot stopped using short focal lengths because the images they produced were too tiny to enjoy. The one-inch-square pictures looked to Talbot like they had been drawn by "some Lilliputian artist." Because Talbot used paper negatives, he was not able to make clear enlargements. With motion picture film, Barnack could. Thanks to this breakthrough, Barnack was able to take Talbot's idea one step further. He had built a better "mousetrap."

With the 35mm camera, amateurs could produce images that rivaled those produced with professional equipment. As a result, many amateurs began to pay more attention to the craft of picture taking. Beginning in the 1930s, high schools and colleges began to offer classes in photography, just as they did for other arts and crafts. Amateur photography became not just a way to create keepsakes, but a hobby to pursue for a lifetime.

The Advent of Color

Amateur photography became even more popular thirteen years after the Leica was introduced. In 1938, the Eastman Kodak Company began to sell the first low-cost color film. This film was known as Kodachrome.

From the very beginning of photography, inventors had tried to find ways to reproduce the colors of nature. As early as 1861, a British physicist named James Clerk Maxwell had devised a way of projecting three photographic images—each a different color—onto a screen. The three images overlapped, so the three colors mixed on the screen, producing a

In 1938, the Eastman Kodak Company began to sell the first low-cost color film. (Above) A color picture of children fishing in the bayous of Louisiana, taken in 1940 by Walcott. (Left) A 1939 Walcott photograph of three people fishing near Belzone, Mississippi.

THE FIRST COLOR FILM

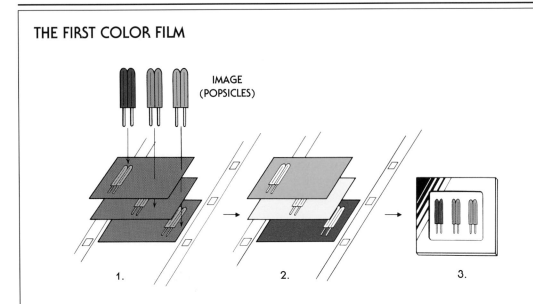

IMAGE
(POPSICLES)

1.　　　　2.　　　　3.

1. In 1938, Kodachrome slide film be-came the first commercially developed color film. Color film is made by coating camera film with three different layers of silver salts. One layer is sensitive only to red light, so that wherever red hits the film, it forms a silver image on this layer. Another layer is sensitive only to blue, and the third layer is sensitive only to green. Combinations of these three primary colors can create every color in the world. After the film is ex-posed and developed, each layer will contain a different silver image, de-pending on the different amounts of red, blue, and green in the subject photographed.

2. The color film then goes through a second development process. This time, color dyes are added to cover the entire surface of each layer *except* where the silver images are. A cyan, or bluish green, dye is added to the layer with the image formed by red light. A yellow dye surrounds the image made by blue light, and a magenta, or bluish red, dye surrounds the image formed by green light.

Finally, the silver is bleached out of the original images on each layer, leav-ing transparent areas wherever the silver images had been. The resulting nega-tive contains one layer covered with cyan dye, except where the original image was formed by red light, one layer covered with yellow dye, except where blue light had formed an image, and a third layer covered with magenta dye, except where the layer was origi-nally exposed to green.

3. When these three layers are mounted together, they form the fin-ished slide. When white light, which is really a combination of the primary col-ors, shines through the slide, each dye filters out certain colors. The layer dyed with cyan filters out all red, except in the transparent spaces originally formed by red light. The yellow layer filters out all blue, except in the transparent spaces originally formed by blue, and the ma-genta layer filters out green, except where green had formed the transpar-ent image. As a result, the viewer sees a mixture of red, blue, and green just as they appeared in the original subject.

Color film captures the full spectrum of color, from violet to red, by using three layers of emulsion. One layer records red light, one records green light, and one records blue light. These three colors—red, green, and blue—can be combined to create every color imaginable.

full-color effect. Seven years later, a French inventor named Louis Ducos du Hauron found a way of creating colored images on paper. Neither of these methods produced colors that were fully lifelike, however.

The Kodachrome method did produce vivid, real colors. Developed by Leopold Mannes and Leopold Godowsky, Kodachrome film was coated with three thin layers of emulsion. Each layer was sensitive to a different color of light. One layer responded only to red. Another layer responded only to green. A third layer responded only to blue. Mannes and Godowsky knew that these three colors can be combined to create every color visible to the human eye. By recording different amounts of these three colors, the Kodachrome negative was able to capture the full range of colors in any scene.

The vivid colors produced by Kodachrome film changed all of photography, especially home photography.

Kodachrome itself is a slide film. In other words, it forms positive color transparencies. These images must be placed in a special viewer or be projected onto a screen for viewing. But the principles of the invention were soon used to produce low-cost color print film.

Once color print film became affordable, most amateurs preferred to use it. Its realness surpassed even that of black-and-white film. With color film, grass was green, the sky was blue, and a red dress appeared red. Color film recorded colors as they were, while black-and-white film changed them to something else.

Most amateurs prefer to use color film because of the added realness of the image. Everything from plants to people are recorded in tones close to their natural colors.

Instant Photography

Black-and-white photography made something of a comeback in home photography in the 1940s. This change was caused, in part, by a child. One day in 1943, an American named Edwin H. Land was taking pictures of his daughter. She wanted to see the pictures right away. Land told her that the pictures would not be ready for about two weeks. His daughter was not satisfied. Neither was he. Why should there be a wait? he thought. Why could there not be such a thing as an instant picture?

Land began to work on instant photography. He searched for the chemicals that were most sensitive to light and a way to develop them quickly. His solution became known as Polaroid film. It consisted of sheets of highly

People around the world take more than fifty billion pictures each year, often recording moments of great personal meaning.

sensitive film held in a cartridge at the back of the camera. After exposing a sheet, the user removed it from the camera. After about a minute, the fast-acting dyes had formed the image. When Polaroid film was first introduced in 1948, the user had to apply chemicals to the print to fix it. Later Polaroid film did not require the fixing step.

Instant photography was easy, fast, and fun. Millions of Polaroid Land cameras were sold in the 1950s and 1960s. In 1963, the Polaroid Corporation introduced Polacolor, the world's first instant color film. With color, instant photography became even more popular.

Today, cameras are found in more than 93 percent of American homes. People around the world take more than fifty billion pictures each year—ten pictures for every man, woman, and child on the planet. The vast majority of these pictures are taken at family events in and around the home. Some are funny. Some are sad. All mean something to someone. None can be replaced.

CHAPTER 8

A Fine Art

"From this day, painting is dead!" exclaimed the French artist Paul Delaroche when Daguerre's first photographs were presented at the joint session of the French Academies of Sciences and Fine Arts in 1839. Delaroche was wrong, of course. Artists did not stop painting in 1839. But Delaroche was partly right. A certain kind of painting did begin to die when photography was invented. Oddly enough, this type of painting was developed at the same time as the camera obscura, and perhaps because of it.

Realism Comes to Art

Before the invention of the camera obscura, most art did not portray the world as the eye saw it. Art was used to decorate things, to express feelings, to portray ideas, and to reveal unseen worlds. Few artists depicted objects exactly as they appear in nature.

This began to change around 1300, about a century after Ibn al-Haitham's findings about light, sight, and pinhole images began to spread through Europe. During this time, known as the Renaissance, artists like Duccio, Giotto, and Pietro Lorenzetti began to make the scenes in their paintings look like those in nature. Describing Lorenzetti's 1343 painting *The Birth of the Virgin,* the art historian H. W. Janson wrote, "Only now does the picture surface assume the quality of a transparent window through which—not *on* which—we perceive the same kind of space we know from daily experience."

Later Renaissance artists like Leonardo da Vinci used science to make their paintings even more faithful to nature. To capture the true form of animals, da Vinci often cut them apart and studied their inner structure. He also attended human surgeries and autopsies to find out about the workings of the human body. When it came to understanding perspective, or how objects appeared at a distance, da Vinci used the camera obscura.

Leonardo da Vinci and other Renaissance artists used the camera obscura to create realistic perspective in their art.

Early photographic artists often used models and props to imitate scenes like those found in popular paintings, as in this photograph by William Lake Price, Don Quixote in His Study.

Art and the Camera Obscura

Da Vinci and others began to formulate strict rules about perspective, based on what they learned from the camera obscura.

The portable camera obscura helped many artists paint even more realistic pictures. This type of painting became known as realism. Realism remained the most widely practiced style of painting for three hundred years.

When photography was first introduced, it was seen by some as offering the ultimate in realism. "Daguerre's process," wrote Paul Delaroche, "completely satisfies all the demands of art, carrying certain essential principles of art to such perfection that it must be a subject of observation and study even to the most accomplished painters."

Not everyone agreed with Delaroche. Another French painter, Jean-Auguste-Dominique Ingres, was one of several artists who signed a formal protest in 1862 that called photography a mechanical process that could not be "compared with those works which are the fruits of intelligence and the study of art."

Photography Imitates Art

To prove that photography could be as much an art as painting, many early photographers tried to make their pictures look like paintings. For example, the great American painter Thomas Eakins often hired models to dress in unusual clothing and pose as they might for a painting. Eakins then photographed the models. Some of these pictures were quite interesting, but others looked sort of silly. The models in his photograph *Two Girls in Greek Dress* convey a certain air of mystery, but they also look a bit like children playing dress-up.

The problem with the painterly approach to photography was that the eye of the camera was too truthful. The realness of the image tended to spoil the romantic mood the artist tried to create. Even when all the details were carefully planned, as in William Lake Price's photograph *Don Quixote in His Study,* they worked against the desired effect. The scene simply looks too real to pass for a picture of a romantic hero. The viewer tends to think not of Don Quixote, the knight of Miguel de Cervantes's novel, but of Price's model, sitting in a studio surrounded by all kinds of interesting objects.

Attacking the Negative

To make their work seem more "artistic," some late nineteenth century photographers declared war on photographic detail. Their weapon was the painter's tool: the paintbrush. Dipping the brush in silver salts, photographic artists like Alvin Langdon Coburn and Robert Demachy attacked the negative, blotting out details and adding light where it was needed. The results were often hauntingly beautiful, as in Demachy's photograph *Behind the Scenes* and Coburn's 1915 work *Harbor Scene.*

The photographers who changed, or retouched, their photographs to make them look more like paintings were known as pictorialists. Describing the Pictorialist movement, one critic wrote, "Photographers do not copy nature anymore; they interpret it." The American photographer Alfred Stieglitz said the photographer was free "to use any means upon a negative of paper to attain the desired end."

External Scenes Equal Internal Feelings

Beginning in the 1890s, Stieglitz changed his thinking. Instead of altering the negative to create an effect, he began to

Alfred Stieglitz freed photography from both realism and pictorialism by searching for external scenes that matched his internal moods, as in this image, The Terminal.

Stieglitz and his followers practiced "straight" photography, that is, they did not retouch their photographic prints to make the images more appealing. Pictured here is Stieglitz's Venetian Boy.

search harder for everyday scenes that by themselves evoked certain feelings. Stieglitz roamed the streets of New York and Paris, searching for external scenes that matched his inner emotions. "When I see something that serves as an equivalent for what I am experiencing myself," he wrote, "then I feel compelled to set down a picture of it as an honest statement— which statement may be said to represent my feelings about life."

It did not matter what was in the scene, only that it expressed how Stieglitz felt. Stieglitz found that familiar objects often evoked the strongest feelings. Describing his photograph *The Terminal*, Stieglitz wrote:

> There was snow on the ground. A driver in a rubber coat was watering his steaming horses. There seemed to be

something closely related to my deepest feeling in what I saw, and I decided to photograph what was within me. The steaming horses and their driver watering them on a cold winter day; my feeling of aloneness in my own country, amongst my own people.... I felt how fortunate the horses were to have at least a human being to give them the water they needed. What made me see the watering of the horses as I did was my own loneliness.

Stieglitz had a tremendous impact on the art of photography. His notion of "equivalents" freed photography from both realism and pictorialism. A photograph no longer had to be faithful to nature, nor did it have to look like a painting. It could just be itself. The only thing that mattered was that the work expressed or conveyed a feeling, attitude, or vision of life.

The Photo-Secession

Stieglitz founded a camera club dedicated to his ideals of photography. This group was known as the Photo-Secession because most of its members had seceded from, or left, the Camera Club of New York. Stieglitz edited the Photo-Secession's journal, called *Camera Notes*. In 1905, Stieglitz and the Photo-Secession established a gallery dedicated to photographic art. Located at 291 Fifth Avenue in New York City, the gallery became known simply as 291.

Stieglitz published and exhibited the work of others who shared his views on photography, including Paul Strand, Edward Steichen, Edward Weston, and Ansel Adams. Like Stieglitz, each of these photographers took pictures of recognizable things, but they strove to

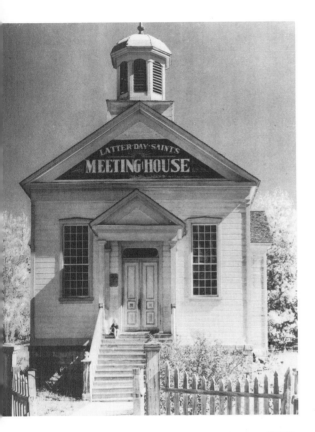

make "a statement that goes beyond the subject," as Ansel Adams put it. They believed in taking "straight" pictures, that is, they refused to retouch their photographs. However, they would use their knowledge of exposure times and developing techniques to create images that matched how they felt about the scene they photographed. For example, Ansel Adams said that as he looked at a scene, he imagined how it would appear in a photographic print. If the image in his mind excited him, he would photograph the scene. He called this process visualization:

> While the landscapes that I have photographed in Yosemite are recognized by most people and, of course, the subject is an important part of the pictures, they are not "realistic." Instead, they are an imprint of my visualization. I want a picture to reflect not only the forms, but what I had seen and

(Above) Ansel Adams used light and shadows to compose beautiful photographs that have influenced the lives of people everywhere. In the photograph at right, Stieglitz uses strong window light and the stark shadows cast by Venetian blinds to create a scene of great mood and feeling.

felt at the moment of the exposure. My *Moonrise, Hernandez, New Mexico* has the emotion and the feeling that the experience of seeing the actual moonrise created in me, but it is not at all realistic. People have asked me why the sky is so dark, thinking exactly in terms of the literal. But the dark sky is how it *felt*.

"A Secret About a Secret"

Guided by their emotions, photographers in the twentieth century have explored all kinds of ways of picturing their feelings about the world around them. Declaring that photography is "a secret about a secret," a photographer named Diane Arbus turned her camera on oddly dressed, deformed, and grotesque human beings to reveal the darker mysteries of our world. Photographers like Herbert Bayer, Ruth Bernhard, Yasuzo Nojima, and Jerry M. Uelsmann abandoned straightforward photography altogether to create images that match their private visions. Like the pictorialists, these photographers cut their negatives apart or made overlapping prints to create wildly imaginary scenes. Photographers like Francis Brugiere, Aaron Siskind, Harry Callahan, and others focused on portions of objects to create almost completely abstract forms. Lotte Jacobi, among others, used the contact print process and other cameraless techniques to create completely abstract images.

Beginning in the 1970s, the general public began to show an increased respect for photography. For example, after Jimmy Carter was elected president in 1976, he selected Ansel Adams to take his official presidential portrait. It was the first time in U.S. history that the official portrait was a photograph, not a painting. At about the same time, the value of original photographic prints began to soar. A large print of *Moonrise, Hernandez, New Mexico,* which Adams had sold ten years before for around $200, was sold at an auction in 1978 for $71,500. One hundred and fifty years after its invention, photography had become widely accepted as a fine art.

An Instrument of Science

When François Arago presented Niépce and Daguerre's discovery to a joint assembly of the French Academies of Sciences and Fine Arts on January 7, 1839, he knew that the uses of the new device would be many and varied. "When inventors of a new instrument apply it to the observations of nature," he commented, "the hopes that they place upon it are always insignificant when compared with the number of subsequent discoveries of which the instrument was the origin." He could not have been more correct.

Photography has revealed corners of the universe otherwise invisible to the human eye. Cameras have gathered light from distant stars and peered deep inside the human body. They have stopped motion that would otherwise be a blur. They have visited the depths of the oceans and recorded the inner workings of atomic particles. Photography has made the impossible possible.

Observing the Heavens

The first scientific use of photography was to observe the heavens. This was only fitting. After all, pinhole images had been used since ancient times as a means of viewing solar eclipses. On July 17, 1850, William Cranch Bond, director of the Harvard College Observatory, and a photographer named John Adams Whipple placed a daguerreotype plate at the eye end of a fifteen-inch telescope. They pointed the telescope at the star Vega and opened the lens, making the first photograph of a star other than the sun.

Astronomers soon found that photographic plates were able to record things the eye could not see. The reason was exposure length. A daguerreotype plate exposed to the sky for about a minute would record pretty much what the eye would see. Exposed for longer than that, it would begin to record light too faint for the eye to see. With long exposures, astronomers were able to peer into deep space for the first time.

Amazing Discoveries

What they saw amazed them. Photographs revealed many more stars in the Milky Way galaxy than anyone had imagined—over 200 billion.

In the 1920s, astronomers discovered that a patch of fuzzy light in the constellation Andromeda was not a cloud of gas, as some scientists had thought, but a galaxy like the Milky Way, containing another 300 billion stars. It appeared faint because it was more than two million light years away. Later images showed that there are countless galaxies even farther away, each containing tens of billions of stars. Photography had enlarged the known universe beyond comprehension.

When scientists turned their cameras toward the heavens, they saw many things they had never seen before. (Above) A photograph of the night sky reveals a spiral galaxy made up of millions of stars. (Below) A photograph of the sun during a total eclipse shows the corona, the bright ring of energy that surrounds the sun.

Photography also helped expand the size of the solar system. Shortly after photography was invented, astronomers knew from their use of the telescope that there were eight planets in the solar system. After years of careful observation, astronomers noticed motions in the orbits of the most distant planets, Uranus and Neptune, that could not be explained. Many scientists concluded that the motions were caused by the gravitational force of an even more distant planet. Astronomers began to search for the unknown planet. The tool they used was the camera.

In 1894, an astronomer named Percival Lowell built an observatory in Arizona and began to photograph the sky. He aimed his camera at an area where he thought the unknown planet should be. Lowell hoped to find the planet by comparing photographs of the same region of sky taken at different times. If any object in the photograph moved, it could not be a star. It would have to be a planet.

Lowell took thousands of photographs without finding anything. He died in 1916 without discovering the planet he was certain existed. One of Lowell's assistants, Clyde Tombaugh, continued the search. Years passed with no success. Then, on February 18, 1930, Tombaugh noticed something unusual.

Tombaugh placed two photographs taken one week apart into a special viewer. The device showed first one photograph, then another, in rapid succession. The pictures were aligned so each star appeared in the same place. As he flipped from one photograph to the other, two tiny dots blinked on and off. When he looked at the pictures closely, he found that a faint object that appeared in one place on the first photograph was showing up in a different place on the second photograph. Since it was moving, the object could not be a star. It was the unknown planet, later named Pluto.

Scientists also used the camera to explore other objects in the solar system, including the sun. On August 7, 1869, Prof. Edward Charles Pickering of Mount Pleasant, Iowa, took the first pictures of a total solar eclipse. Pickering's photographs revealed the exact shape of the great halo, known as the corona, that surrounds the sun. Later photographs showed jets of solar matter rising from the surface of the sun. These plumes of material became known as solar prominences.

This view of the sun, taken with a solar telescope on board the spacecraft Skylab *in 1973, shows a solar prominence shooting out from the surface of the sun.*

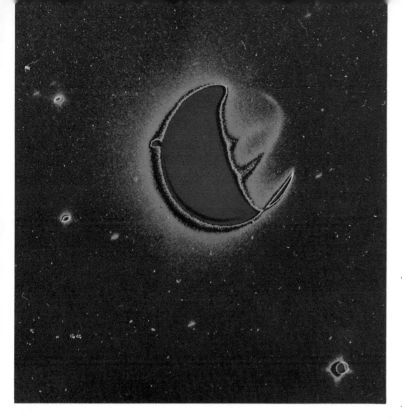

This is a color enhancement of a photograph of earth taken with an ultraviolet camera by John W. Young during the Apollo 16 mission to the moon. The image shows the sunlit atmosphere that surrounds the earth. The bulge on the left side of the planet is light from a background star.

Microscopic Photography

Meanwhile, other scientists began to use the camera to record objects too tiny to observe even with a microscope. These scientists placed cameras on the most powerful microscopes available, then made long exposures to capture as much light reflected by tiny objects as possible. Using this method, scientists were able to take clear pictures of things that looked fuzzy to the human eye.

One of the great microscopic photographs was made on the 110th anniversary of Arago's announcement of Daguerre's invention. On January 7, 1949, Drs. Daniel Chapin Pease and Richard Freligh Baker of the University of Southern California in Los Angeles took the first photograph of human genes. These particles, which transmit physical traits from one generation to another, had to be magnified 120,000 times to be seen.

Objects too small to be seen even with a microscope could still be photographed, scientists learned. They found that when atomic particles collided, they released a burst of energy that would appear as a streak on film. By studying the size, location, and brightness of these streaks, physicists were able to deduce the size and makeup of the unseen particles.

Photographing Energy

Scientists also learned that cameras could record forms of energy invisible to the human eye. One thousand years after Ibn al-Haitham tried to explain what light was, scientists finally were able to describe it in detail. Early in the twentieth century, physicist Albert Einstein found that light is a form of electromagnetic energy that moves in waves. When these waves measure between 400 and

700 nanometers (nm) long (a nanometer is one billionth of a meter), the energy appears as visible light. Wavelengths shorter than 400 nm are known as ultraviolet light. Wavelengths longer than 700 nm are known as infrared light. By using special lens filters, film, and light, cameras can record both ultraviolet and infrared light.

Ultraviolet photography is often used in medical examinations to analyze human tissue. Ultraviolet photography is also used to inspect documents to make certain they are genuine.

Infrared photography can be used to record heat. Since heat penetrates objects, infrared is able to "see" through surfaces to the heat below. Because living matter gives off heat, infrared photography is often used to distinguish between living and nonliving materials. Infrared photographs taken from the air can reveal soldiers hidden by camouflage. An infrared photograph of a planet will show the presence of different gases in the planet's atmosphere.

Photography in Medicine

One of the most helpful uses of photography has been to record electromagnetic energy of very high frequency known as X rays. A form of radiation, X rays pass with ease through many substances. Scientists found that when they place an object between a source of X rays and a photographic plate, a shadowy image of the object appears on the plate. The portions of the object that absorb few X rays appear as a dark area on the negative. Areas that absorb more X rays appear lighter. The process of making an image with X rays is known as radiography.

Doctors soon realized that radiography could be used to "see" inside human bodies. When a human being is exposed to X rays, the flesh does not absorb many of the rays. As a result, flesh appears dark on the film. Bones absorb many more X rays than flesh, so they appear much lighter on the film. If a person has a piece of metal, such as a filling in a tooth, inside his or her body, the metal object will absorb all the X rays that strike it and appear white.

Radiography allows doctors to pinpoint some health problems long before they become visible. For example, cancerous tissue absorbs X rays at a dif-

In an X ray of lungs and a rib cage, the X rays pass through the lungs, turning the photographic plate dark. Many X rays are absorbed by the bones, however, so the photographic plate remains less exposed behind them, causing the bones to appear white.

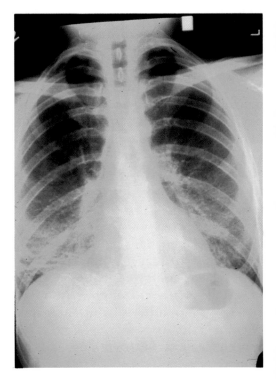

Electronic cameras on board the spacecraft Voyager 2 *recorded images of Saturn and its rings as a pattern of dots, then broadcast the pattern to earth via radio. Computers on earth then assembled the pattern of dots into photographic images.*

ferent rate than healthy tissue does, so cancerous tumors stand out clearly on X rays. Surgeons use this knowledge to find and remove such tumors.

Electronic Imaging

When scientists learned how to break atoms into smaller components in the 1940s, they found that they could use this knowledge to take even clearer pictures. By giving an electrical charge to particles known as electrons, scientists were able to separate them from atoms and aim them at the surface of an object. A device known as an electron microscope fires a beam of such particles at the surface of an object and records the result.

Electron microscopes do not record such images directly on film. Instead, they use sensors that respond to the energy released by the electron bombardment. Electrical pulses given off by the sensors are recorded onto magnetic tape as a series of dots. The tape is then placed in a machine that turns the coded information into an enlarged image that can be recorded on film. The process is known as electronic imaging. Using this method, an electron microscope can magnify an image more than two million times.

Since the electronic image is made up of many dots, it can be transmitted from one point to another via radio waves. Using this principle, it became feasible to place an electronic camera on a spacecraft and send it to a distant world. In 1959, the Soviet Union sent two space probes to the moon. On September 13, 1959, a probe named *Luna 2* beamed many pictures back to earth before crashing into the surface of the moon. One month later, *Luna 3* orbited the moon, sending back the world's first photographs of the far side of the moon.

Cameras aboard later space probes returned close-up pictures of several planets in the solar system, revealing countless features that had never been seen before. In 1974 and 1975, an

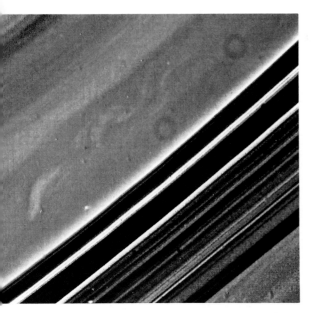

American probe named *Mariner 10* flew within 168 miles of Mercury, showing a surface pocked with craters. In 1976, two American space probes, *Viking I* and *Viking II,* photographed Mars from orbits above the red planet, then landed on its surface. Pioneer and Voyager space probes passed by Mars, Jupiter, Saturn, Uranus, and Neptune. *Voyager I* photographed volcanic activity on Io, one of the moons of Jupiter. It also showed ice fields on Europa, another of Jupiter's moons. *Voyager II* discovered ten moons around Uranus, rings around Neptune, and icy volcanoes on the surface of Neptune's moon, Triton.

(Above) A photograph of Saturn's rings taken by a camera on board Voyager II *reveals features not visible to telescopes on earth. (Below)* Voyager I *took this photograph of Jupiter and two of its satellites, Europa, the white ball near the center of the picture, and Io, the reddish ball on the right side, above Jupiter's Great Red Spot.*

Electronic Photography at Home

The same technology used to record the features of distant planets is now available for use in the home. A computerized camera that senses light electronically and breaks the image into a pattern of dots, a process known as digitizing, was introduced by the Canon Corporation in 1988. The camera is called the Xapshot.

The digitizing process works like this: A tiny computer in the camera stores the digital information for as many as fifty images on a two-inch videodisc. The disc can then be placed into a player that is linked to a computer display or television screen. The image can also be read by a printer that will print the image as a series of dots, similar to a halftone.

Color images can be digitized in the same way, although the equipment used to do so is very expensive and is not available for home use at this time. Using special sensors and laser light, a computerized camera scans an image. It records not only the position, but also the color of each dot. The computer can then store the image on a magnetic disc or a compact disc. The image can be viewed on a color monitor or printed directly onto photographic film or paper.

Once a pattern of dots is stored in a computer's memory, the computer user can change it before making a print. The computer can be used to darken or lighten any portion of an image. The computer can even change the values of the colors, making a red more intense or a blue more pale. Using a process known as anamorphic enlargement, the image can be made smaller or larger.

The picture can be turned, reversed, or made to print either as a positive or a negative. The process of altering photographs by computer is known as image manipulation.

Altering Photographs with Computers

Image manipulation is often used in advertising to make products look more attractive. It is also used in publishing to correct images so they will print better. Because image manipulation can create "impossible" scenes, it poses a major challenge to the long-held notion of the realness of the photograph. In a special issue devoted to photojournalism in the fall of 1989, the editors of *Time* magazine wrote:

> Digital imaging systems can make changes that are virtually undetectable. Figures can be shifted, people and things removed from the frame or added. Computer retouching has already become commonplace in the fantasy world of advertising photography. Now many journalists are troubled by the prospect that the practice will creep into the reproduction of news photos.

In the same issue of *Time*, the editors presented a famous photograph that *Time* had retouched on a computer to make it look better. A photograph of the Olympic runner Mary Decker, who had fallen in a race and lost her chances at the Olympic medal, was altered to make the image more dramatic. In the original photograph, the antenna of a walkie-talkie held by a track official jutted out from behind Decker's head. The object was removed from the frame so it

DIGITIZED COLOR PHOTO REPRODUCTION

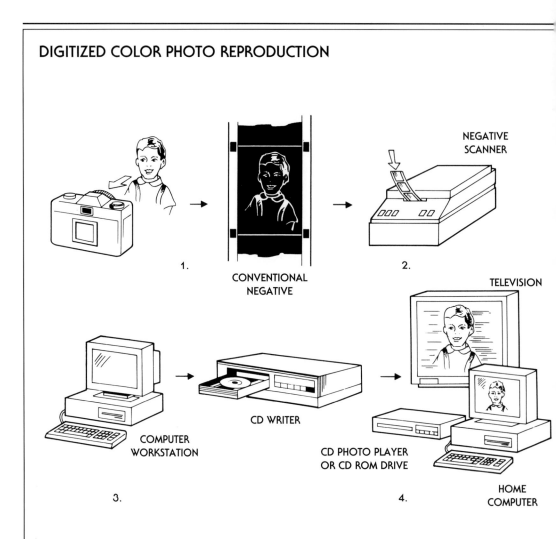

NEGATIVE
SCANNER

1.

CONVENTIONAL
NEGATIVE

2.

TELEVISION

CD WRITER

COMPUTER
WORKSTATION

CD PHOTO PLAYER
OR CD ROM DRIVE

HOME
COMPUTER

3.

4.

A photo compact disc (or CD) system enables its user to view digitized color photos on a television or computer screen, to alter or enhance them on a personal computer, and to merge and print them with other documents. To obtain a digitized photo, one begins with a conventional negative (1). This is fed into a negative scanner, which reads the image and converts it into a digital code (2). This information is transferred to a computer workstation (3), which translates it into special format for a photo CD writer (4). The CD writer uses a laser to imprint the digitized information onto a compact disc. The compact disc can be then inserted into a photo CD player and the photo can be viewed on a television screen. Or it may be used in the CD-ROM drive of a personal computer. With the personal computer, the digitized photo can be enlarged, reduced, enhanced, altered, merged into other documents, printed, or sent to other computers.

This photograph of Olympic runner Mary Decker was retouched to eliminate a flaw in the original. The walkie-talkie antenna that seems to jut out of Decker's head was removed with the help of a computer.

would not detract from the anguished face of the fallen athlete.

By tempting editors to make their pictures a little more exciting and attention getting, electronic imaging poses serious challenges to the ethics of photojournalism. But electronic processes also offer great potential for photographers to achieve completed images that match their inner visions. Before his death, Ansel Adams predicted that electronics would revolutionize photography:

Electronic photography will soon be superior to anything we have now. The first advance will be the exploration of existing negatives. I believe the electronic process will enhance them. I could get superior prints from my negatives using electronics. Then the time will come when you will be able to make the entire photograph electronically. With the extremely high resolution and the enormous control you can get from electronics, the results will be fantastic. I wish I were young again!

Glossary

■ ■

alloy: A mixture of two or more metals.

aperture: A small opening that admits light into a darkened room, box, or camera.

bitumen of Judea: A type of asphalt that hardens when exposed to light.

calotype: A photographic image printed from a paper negative.

camera obscura: A darkened room with a small hole in one wall that admits just enough light rays to form an inverted image on a screen or the opposite wall.

compound: A combination of two or more elements.

concave: Curving inward, as the inside of a hollow sphere. A concave lens is thinner in the center than at the edge.

convex: Curving outward, as the outside of a sphere. A convex lens is thicker in the center than at the edge.

collodion: A clear, syrupy emulsion made from a mixture of cellulose nitrate, ether, and alcohol.

daguerreotype: A photographic image on a silver-coated plate sensitized with silver iodide and developed with mercury vapor.

dry plate: A glass photographic plate coated with an emulsion of gelatin and silver bromide that remains sensitive to light after it has dried.

emulsion: Light-sensitive coating for film, plates, paper, etc., usually consisting of silver salts in gelatin.

enlargement: A photographic print that is larger than the negative from which it was printed.

film: A sheet, roll, or strip of flexible, transparent material, usually celluloid, coated with emulsion.

focal length: The distance from the center of a curved lens or mirror at which light rays converge.

focus: The point at which light rays converge after passing through an aperture or a lens; also the adjustment of a camera lens that produces a clear image.

glass plate negative: A photographic image formed in an emulsion on a glass plate.

halftone: A photographic image composed of many dots made by placing a screen between a photographic plate and the source of light.

heliogravure: A method of engraving a printing plate using direct sunlight to harden a light-sensitive material.

latent image: An invisible image formed in emulsion by exposure to light.

lens: A disc of glass with one or two curved sides capable of bending light.

lithography: A printing process in which a flat surface, such as a stone or metal plate, is chemically treated so that ink adheres only to the portions that are to be printed.

negative: An image produced on a transparent photographic plate or film in which lights and darks are reversed.

negative-positive process: The method of producing a positive photographic image by first making a transparent negative, then shining light through the negative and onto light-sensitive paper.

optics: The study of light and vision.

photoengraving: The process of engraving a printing plate by exposing light-sensitive materials to light.

photograph: An image produced on a light-sensitive surface, such as a chemically treated sheet of paper.

photography: The process of creating images by briefly exposing chemically treated surfaces to light.

pinhole: A small opening; an aperture.

pinhole image: An image formed on a blank surface by light rays that have passed through a small opening.

shutter: A mechanical device that controls the amount of light admitted into a camera.

silver bromide: The chemical compound of silver and bromine, used in dry-plate emulsion.

silver iodide: A chemical compound of silver and iodine, used in daguerreotype emulsion.

silver nitrate: A chemical compound of silver and nitric acid, used in calotype emulsion.

silver salt: Any of a number of light-sensitive chemical compounds containing silver.

sodium chloride: Common salt, used to "fix" early photographs.

spectrum: The visible part of the electromagnetic spectrum; also the band of color formed when white light passes through a prism.

stereoscopy: A method of producing three-dimensional images using a pair of images taken from slightly different angles and viewed through special viewers.

wet-plate photography: A photographic process in which a glass plate is covered with an emulsion of silver nitrate and collodion and exposed while wet.

For Further Reading

Boy Scouts of America, *Photography,* New Brunswick, NJ: Boy Scouts of America, 1956.

Valerie C. Burkig, *Photonics, the New Science of Light.* Hillside, NJ: Enslow Publishers, 1986.

Paul Clement Czaja, *Writing with Light.* Riverside, CN: The Chatham Press, Inc., 1973.

Carl Glassman, *Hocus Focus, The World's Weirdest Cameras.* New York: Franklin Watts, 1976.

Russell Miller, *Click.* New York: Arco Publishing Company, Inc., 1974.

Vick Owens-Knudsen, *Photography Basics.* Englewood Cliffs, NJ: Prentice-Hall, 1983.

Martin W. Sandler, *The Story of American Photography.* Boston: Little, Brown and Company, 1979.

Works Consulted

Paul E. Boucher, *Fundamentals of Photography*. Princeton, NJ: D. Van Nostrand Company, Inc., 1940.

Brian Coe, *The Birth of Photography, the Story of the Formative Years 1800–1900*. New York: Taplinger Publishing Company, 1976.

Brian Coe, *Cameras from Daguerreotypes to Instant Pictures*. New York: Crown Publishers, Inc., 1975.

Douglas Davis, *Photography as a Fine Art*. Boston: Hill & Company, Publishers, 1976.

Leonard Ford and John Hedgecoe, *The Photographer's Handbook*. New York: Alfred A. Knopf, Inc., 1977.

Helmut Gernsheim in collaboration with Alison Gernsheim, *A Concise History of Photography*. New York: Grosset & Dunlap, 1965.

Life Library of Photography. New York: Time-Life Books, 1970.

150 Years of Photojournalism. New York: Time Inc. Magazines, Fall 1989.

Parade, The Sunday Newspaper Magazine. New York: Parade Publications, Inc., June 9, 1991.

John Baptista Porta, *Natural Magick*. New York: Basic Books, Inc., 1957.

Lois Walton Sipley, *Photography's Great Inventors*. Philadelphia: American Museum of Photography, 1965.

Susan Sontag, *On Photography*. New York: Farrar, Straus and Giroux, 1977.

Julia Van Haaften, *From Talbot to Stieglitz*. New York: Thames and Hudson, 1982.

Johann Willsberger, translated by Helga Halaki, *The History of Photography*. New York: Doubleday & Company, Inc., 1977.

Index

About the Author

■ ■

The author of six books for young adults,
Bradley Steffens became keenly interested in
photography through his friendship with Silvia
Salmi, a pioneer in candid portrait photography.
Neighbors in the village of Ajijic, Mexico,
Steffens and Salmi often discussed the art of
photography in the courtyard of the photographer's large home. Looking through Salmi's vast
collection of portraits of well-known people such
as Wallace Stevens, Robert Frost, Diego Rivera,
Eleanor Roosevelt, and Leo Trotsky, Steffens felt
like a silent traveler to a vanished world.

Picture Credits